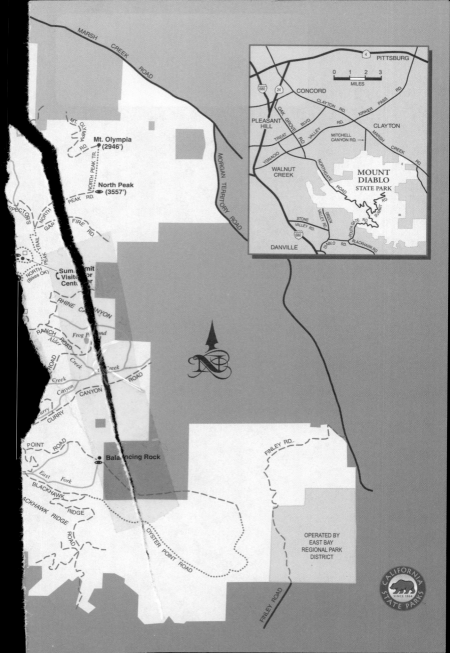

THE

Mount Diablo

GUIDE

SECOND EDITION

THE MOUNT DIABLO INTERPRETIVE ASSOCIATION

BERKELEY HILLS BOOKS

Berkeley, California

Published by Berkeley Hills Books, P.O. Box 9877, Berkeley, CA 94709
www.berkeleyhills.com
Distributed by Publishers Group West

Library of Congress Cataloging-in-Publication Data

The Mount Diablo guide / The Mount Diablo Interpretive Association.—2nd ed.
    p. cm.
Includes index.
    ISBN 1-893163-22-9 (pbk. : alk. paper)
    1. Mount Diablo State Park (Calif.)—Guidebooks. 2. Natural history—California—
Mount Diablo State Park—Guidebooks. I. Mt. Diablo Interpretive Association.
    F868.C76 M68 2002
    917.94'63—dc21

                                    2002010128

Designed by Elysium Design/San Francisco

TABLE OF CONTENTS

preface

We at the Mount Diablo Interpretive Association ("MDIA") are excited about the publication of this book, the first guidebook devoted exclusively to Mount Diablo. On behalf of MDIA's officers and Board of Directors, I would like to thank all of the MDIA volunteers whose hard work and dedication have made this second edition possible.

This book is based in part on pamphlets, articles, and other materials that have been prepared and revised by MDIA volunteers over a period of many years. MDIA owes a great debt to these volunteers. Special mention should go to Keith Patterson, who devoted many hours to assembling background materials and photographs for use in this book; Craig Lyon and Roi Peers, who assisted in the preparation of the chapter on geology; Kevin Hintsa, who contributed much to the chapter on the wildlife of Mt. Diablo; Susan Bazell (deciduous) and Peg Steunenberg (evergreens), who kindly allowed the line drawings of oak trees to reprinted from MDIA's previous publication *Plants of the East Bay Parks;* Ken Lavin, Marjorie Ratner, and Bill Pierson who helped me with the Mitchell Canyon Interpretive Trail Guide; and Frank and Edith Valle-Riestra, two of MDIA's original founders, who helped review a draft of this book. Frank also wrote the short, moderate, and demanding hikes descriptions. Further, MDIA volunteers donated many of the fine photographs in this book.

In addition to MDIA volunteers, we would also like to thank Seth Adams of Save Mount Diablo for reviewing the history chapter, and for permitting his comprehensive timeline of Mt. Diablo's history to be excerpted. Save Mount Diablo is a nonprofit organization devoted to preserving and expanding Mount Diablo State Park through the acquisition of new lands. Thanks also go to Mike McCormack of the Bicycle Trails Council of the East Bay and Laura Tow of the California Horseriders Association.

Finally, I would like to thank Brian Hickey, Park Superintendent of Mount Diablo State Park, and Dave Matthews, former Supervising Ranger, for their assistance and support.

We hope you find this second edition of the guidebook a useful and entertaining aid to your enjoyment of the mountain.

Linda Sanford
Secretary, Mount Diablo Interpretive Association
Chair of the Publications Committee

Mt. Diablo Interpretive Association is a non-profit organization devoted to the promotion of interpretive, scientific, and educational projects to help the general public enjoy and become knowledgeable about Mt. Diablo. The Association also operates the Mitchell Canyon Interpretive Center. For more information on MDIA write to PO Box 346, Walnut Creek, CA 94597-0346, call (925) 927-7222, or go to our website www.mdia.org.

mt. diablo state park general information

Address: Mount Diablo State Park, 96 Mitchell Canyon Road, Clayton, California 94517.
Mount Diablo State Park general information number: (925)837-2525.

To reach South Gate entrance, take the Diablo Road exit off highway 680, take Diablo Road east to Mt. Diablo Scenic Blvd., and turn left. To reach North Gate entrance, take the Ygnacio Valley Road exit off highway 680, take Ygnacio Valley Road east to Walnut Ave. Turn right onto Walnut Ave., then right on Castle Rock Road, then immediately left on North Gate Road. To reach Mitchell Canyon, follow Ygnacio Valley Road to Clayton Rd. (right), then east to Mitchell Canyon Rd. (right), and then south two miles to the entrance.

The park is open every day 8am to sunset. Gates are closed to arriving visitors 45 minutes before sunset. The park is occasionally closed because of fire danger or other hazardous weather. For the latest information on mountain weather conditions, call (925)838-9225. For the latest information on park closure and road conditions, call (925)837-2525.

PARK ADMISSION FEES
Rates vary for camping and day use, senior rates (over 65) are available. Annual Pass (covering all California state parks) is $35. Macedo Ranch parking day permit $2.

Mt. Diablo's Sector Office is located on the right just before the entrance to the Mitchell Canyon parking lot and trailhead. Hours are Monday–Friday, 8am to 5pm. Phone (925)673-2891.

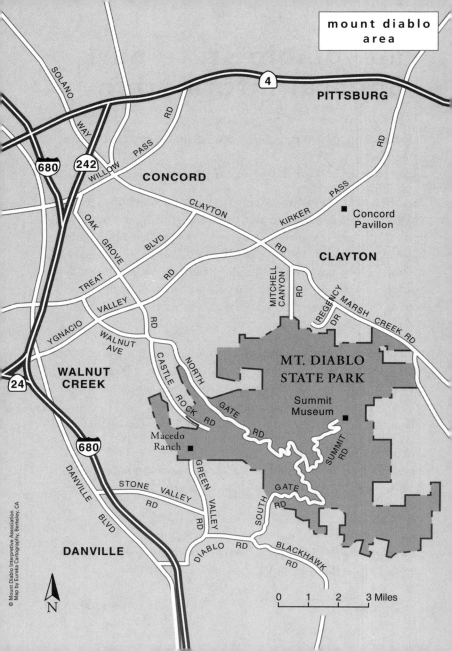

The **Mitchell Canyon Interpretive Center** is located in the parking lot at the south end of Mitchell Canyon Road in Clayton and operated by the Mount Diablo Interpretive Association. The Center is currently open from 8am to 4pm on Saturdays and Sundays, and some holidays; time will vary with the seasons and weather conditions. It has displays about various aspects of Mt. Diablo State Park, such as geology, wildlife, trails, and plant life. Interpretive materials about the Park, such as geology, wildlife, and plants, are on sale. There are also post-cards, note cards, trail maps, and water for sale.

The **Summit Visitor Center** is open Wednesday through Sunday 11am to 5pm during summer months, 10am to 4pm during the winter. Admission to the museum is free. The phone number is (925)837-6119.

No alcoholic beverages are permitted in the park; state laws regarding alcoholic beverages are strictly enforced. Motor homes (RVs) are permitted up to 20 feet in length. Firearms/airguns are prohibited. There is no hunting allowed in the park. Fireworks are not allowed. Skateboards, rollerskates, rollerblades, and other gravity-propelled devices are also prohibited. Dogs are permitted, but must be kept in a tent or vehicle at night, and be on leash at all times when out of the car or tent. They are allowed in developed areas only—not allowed on trails or fire roads. Rock climbing is allowed, and popular in the Rock City and Castle Rock areas. Hang gliding and paragliding are permitted off the summit of the mountain (lower summit parking lot). Hang gliders and paragliders must have a permit.

Mt. Diablo State Park has over sixty **campsites**. There are five group campsites: Stagecoach, Boundary, Buckeye, Wildcat, and BBQ Terrace. Stagecoach has a capacity of 20 people and 7 cars—no RVs. Boundary has a capacity of 20 people and 7 cars—no RVs. BBQ Terrace has a capacity of 50 people and 17 cars (no RVs). Buckeye and Wildcat both have a capacity of 30 people and 10 cars (no RVs). Check with the park for current fees.

A group campground suitable for horses is located at BBQ Terrace, with stalls for 50 horses. You can trailer your horse into this site, which has water troughs, picnic tables, barbecue stoves and pit toilets. The site can be reserved by contacting park headquarters.

All group camping is on the reservation system. Group camping reservations can be made year round through Reserve America Reservation Company: (800)444-7275 or www.reserveamerica.com. All unreserved sites are available on a first-come, first-served basis. The sites will rarely fill up except under exceptional weather conditions and on occasional weekends and holidays. Persons under 18 must have written permission from their parents to camp in the park. Quiet hours are 10pm to 6am. No electric generators from 8pm to 10am. There are restrictions on the use of fires during fire season; check with the ranger. All fires must be in stoves or the barbecues provided—no ground fires. Firewood gathering is prohibited. Noise must not carry beyond your immediate camp or picnic site. Public telephones are located at the Mitchell Canyon parking area, Junction headquarters, Macedo Ranch, and the Summit Visitor Center.

Three campgrounds—Live Oak, Junction, and Juniper—have restrooms, and Live Oak and Juniper also have hot showers. Live Oak has 22 sites—a site consisting of a parking space, picnic table, and fire ring or barbecue grill. Junction has 6 sites, Juniper 36. Camping is permitted for a maximum of 8 persons and 2 vehicles per campsite in the Juniper, Junction, and Live Oak campgrounds. These sites can be reserved by calling Reserve America Reservation Company at (800)444-7275.

There are over 25 picnic areas on the mountain. All have picnic tables, most have restrooms and running water. For picnic reservations dial (925) 837-0904. The following is a list of picnic areas in the order they are reached when traveling toward the summit from the South Gate entrance. The name of the picnic area is followed by the facilities to be found there:

Lower Rock City Area
5 well-spaced picnic tables each with their own barbecue pit, a shared barrel burner, and water.

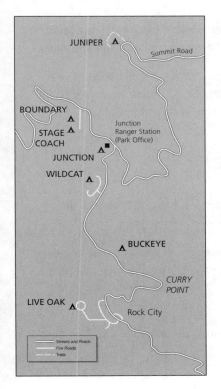

Uplands Picnic Area
2 picnic tables, barbecue pit, and water.

Upper Rock City
Scattered single picnic tables.

Artist Point Picnic Area
1 table, barbecue pit, pit toilets and water.

Little Rock Picnic Area
Up stone steps there is a table. Behind the large boulder is another table, barbecue pit and water.

Grotto Picnic Area
2 separate tables, 2 barbecue pits and water.

Upper Arroyo Picnic Area
A more private area with a

picnic table, barbecue pit, and water.

Lower Arroyo Picnic Area
Across the road from the Arroyo Picnic Area is a more secluded area with a picnic table, barbecue pit, pit toilet, and water.

Horseshoe Picnic Area
At the upper right there is one picnic table, a pit toilet and water. On the upper left there is one table and a barbecue pit. The middle site has one picnic table, pit toilet, and barbecue pit.

Bridal Nook Picnic Area
Located 3.2 miles above South Gate kiosk is a private picnic table nested under the trees. There is a barbecue pit, small stream and water.

Maple Nook Picnic Area
Located 3.4 miles above South Gate kiosk is another private picnic table with barbecue pit, small stream and water.

Junction Picnic Area
2 tables, 2 barbecue pits, and water.

Canyon Nook Picnic Area
Located just past Junction with picnic table, and barbecue pit.

Sunset Picnic Area
To the left is one large and one small picnic table, barbecue pit and pit toilets. Turning right will lead you to two more secluded picnic tables set apart from one another, two barbecue pits, and water.

Rocky Point Picnic Area
5 picnic tables, 4 barbecue pits, l grill, pit toilet and water.

Lookout Point Picnic Area

2 separated picnic tables (one as you drive into the parking area, the other at the top of a knoll at lookout). Each picnic table has a barbecue pit and there is water.

The Pines Picnic Area
2 picnic tables, 2 barbecue pits, and water.

Round Top Picnic Area
Fantastic view, 1 picnic table, barbecue pit, and water.

Toyon Picnic Area
1 picnic table, 1 grill, and pit toilet.

Blue Oak Picnic Area
3 picnic tables, 1 grill, a barbecue pit, and pit toilets.

Oak Knoll Picnic Area
6 separate picnic tables (3 with grills, 3 with barbecue pits). Water and pit toilets are available.

Grapevine Picnic Area
Three miles above the Junction Station is a picnic table nestled under the trees with a barbecue pit.

Laurel Dell Group Picnic Area
9 picnic tables, a large barbecue pit, pit toilets, water, and a water fountain.

Muir Picnic Area
3 picnic tables, 2 barbecue pits, pit toilets, and water.

Lower Summit Parking Lot
8 picnic tables overlooking Livermore Valley along the parking lot rim. Flush toilets nearby.

Sunrise from the summit building. ©*Tom Paiva*.

Mt. Diablo, late afternoon. ©*Tom Paiva.*

highlights of mount diablo state park

the view

Of the park's more than 1 million annual visitors, it is estimated that about half head straight for the summit to enjoy the spectacular view.

Over the years, many large claims have been made for the view, some controversial. Josiah Whitney—for whom Mt. Whitney is named—estimated that the view from the summit was equivalent to the area of all six New England states combined. Others have claimed (more modestly) that it equals the area of New York State. It is generally allowed that more land and water can be seen from atop Diablo than from any other peak in the contiguous United States. Given that it is not a particularly tall peak, what accounts for Diablo's vista? Two things: the flatness of the surrounding territory (Delta, Bay, San Ramon and Central Valley), and the gradual rise of the Sierra in the east, which brings higher points into view as the distance increases, and offsets the curvature of the earth.

In recent years, haze has decreased visibility from the summit. The best viewing is on crisp winter mornings, immediately after rains have scoured the air. The bigger the storm, the better the prospect the following morning. Among the features indisputably on view at such times are, to the north: Mt Lassen (10,466 ft elev., 165 miles away) and (closer in) Suisun Bay, the Carquinez Straits (23 miles) and much of the Delta; in the east, the Central Valley (called the San Joaquin here), over 400 miles of the Sierra, and Half Dome in Yosemite. To the south:

Photo taken March 1956. 38 miles to San Francisco. 72 miles to the Farallons (in the

distant left). Horizon is about 125 miles distant. *Courtesy Contra Costa Historical Society.*

Livermore valley, Mt Hamilton (4213 ft.—about 40 miles), and Mt. Loma Prieta in the Santa Cruz Mountains (3,791 ft). In the west can be seen the San Ramon valley, the Berkeley hills, San Francisco Bay with its bridges, the Golden Gate (28 miles), and Mt. Tamalpais (2600 ft). The Farallons (60 miles) are usually obscured by fog but can be made out on exceptionally clear days. Summit elevation is 3849'. Other selected elevations in the park: Mitchell Canyon parking lot— 600', Mitchell Rock—1080', Twin Peaks—1733', Eagle Peak—2369', Juniper Campground—2900', Rock City—1600', North Peak—3557'.

summit museum

The most significant and largest man-made structure on Mt. Diablo is the summit museum building and observation tower. It was constructed in 1939–1942 by the Civilian Conservation Corps. Plans for the building had begun in 1934, and were developed and elaborated over the next five years. It is a fine example of National Park Service rustic architecture. The rock was quarried from Mt. Diablo itself (from Fossil Ridge).

The summit of Mt. Diablo is actually inside the museum building. Here is also located the brass monument marking the axis of the first geodetic survey of California (1851).

The museum has a diorama of the park's various ecosystems. A model of the mountain acquaints visitors with important park locations. Panels on the lower level describe the Native American history of the region. A rock wall with instructional video examines the geological forces that created the mountain. Rotating displays of interpretive art by local artists and photographers complement the permanent exhibits. The museum also features a gift shop and audio-visual room.

Outside, telescopes are mounted on the observation deck to help enjoy the vista. On the walk up the circular stairway to the observation deck, look for ancient marine fossils embedded in the sandstone walls of the building. In the rotunda visitors are reminded of Mt. Diablo's importance as a survey point. Above the rotunda is a beacon, historically important to aviators and now lighted once a year on December 7 in memory of Pearl Harbor survivors.

The museum is open from 11am to 5pm during the summer months and 10am to 4pm during the winter, Wednesday through Sunday and on holidays. Admission is free. Phone (925)837-6119 to confirm opening hours and days.

stargazing

The Mount Diablo Observatory Association (MDOA), a volunteer organization, provides regularly scheduled public programs on the summit of Mt. Diablo with telescopes set up to view celestial objects. All the programs are at the lower summit parking lot, and are weather permitting; fog, heavy overcast, or rain can cancel without prior notice. Be sure to dress warmly (in layers), and bring a flashlight with a *red* lens. Program begins at sunset and usually ends by 11pm. Exit, at the end of the program, is through North Gate only. For schedule of programs call (925)691-6362; or visit their website: http://members.aol.com/mdas101b/private/members.htm.

rock city

A mile from the Danville entrance along South Gate Road, Rock City features sandstone rock formations that have been weathered by wind and rain into miniature turrets, caves and grottos. One of the most prominent is Elephant Rock, near the entrance to Live Oak Campground. Sentinel Rock is Rock City's tallest and provides a good view of Diablo's peak. It is about 15 minutes by foot from the parking area. Another 10 minutes up the trail leads to Wind Caves.

Rock City is one of the Bay Area's most popular sites for climbing, offering climbs up to 80 feet in height. Rocks suitable for scaling can be found on either side of South Gate Road. Amazing Face, a rock on the lower tier, is one of the most popular because it has bolts at the top to secure ropes. Bolts are not installed or maintained by park staff or state employees. New bolts are not to be installed in any rock within the park boundaries, and caution should be exercised when using any bolt or other projection while climbing. The grills and picnic tables in Rock City were built by the Civilian Conservation Corps in the 1930s.

cultural history
of mt. diablo

native americans and mount diablo

Native people have lived within sight of Diablo for at least 5,000 years. The mountain is in the ethnographic territory of the Bay Miwok Indians. This territory extended through the eastern portions of Contra Costa County northeast to the Sacramento–San Joaquin Delta. The Bay Miwok spoke a Penutian dialect distinct from the language of other Miwok peoples. The aboriginal population at its greatest is estimated at around 1700.

Five tribelets of individual political units have been identified for the Bay Miwok: the Scanlon, Volvon, Chupcan, Julpun, and Ompin. The Volvon (also called Wolwon or Bolbon) lived closest to Mount Diablo. Early Spanish explorers refer to the mountain as Cerro Alto de los Bolbones. Their principal village was located at the mountain's southeast base. They lived in homes constructed of willow frames thatched with tule and native bunchgrasses and shaped like upside-down bowls. The fall months were spent in the oak-covered hills, gathering acorns for storage, the winter in villages, the spring and summer moving through the area gathering food and hunting.

Like other California groups, the Bay Miwok were intensive food collectors. The more important plant foods included acorns, Foothill and Coulter pine seeds, seeds from various grasses and plants, and Brodiaea bulbs—all of which are abundant on Mount Diablo. Acorns were the single most important food source in aboriginal California.

Blue oak, valley oak, and coast live oak—three species plentiful on Mount Diablo—produced the acorns most commonly used by the natives.

Permanent Indian villages were restricted to the foot of the mountain. The higher slopes were never occupied, but natives would visit there to pray and perform rituals. Several of these Native American groups also honored the mountain in their mythology. In a Plains Miwok creation account, Mol-luk (Condor-man) lived on the north side of Mt. Diablo. His wife, the rock on which he roosted, gave birth to Wek-wek (Prairie falcon-man). With the help of his grandfather, Coyote-man, Wek-wek created the Indian people, providing them with everything they needed to live.

Most of the Volvons were removed to the San Jose Mission in 1805–1806.

Dr. Randall Frost, the avid hiker and nationally published journalist, recorded one of several Miwok legends relating to Mt. Diablo:

How Tol-Le-Loo Stole Fire
Long ago the chiefs of the [San Joaquin] Valley People were Wek-wek the Falcon and We-pi-ah-gah the Golden Eagle. Their neighbors to the east, the Mountain People, lived in darkness in the Sierra Nevada. Although they wanted fire, they did not know where or how to obtain it. O-la-choo, the Coyote-man, tried to find it but failed. Eventually Tol-le-loo the White-footed Mouse found out that the Valley People had fire, and O-la-choo sent him to steal it.

Taking his elderberry flute with him, Tol-le-loo travelled west until he reached the home of the Valley people. Arriving outside their round-house, Tol-le-loo sat down and began to play his flute. Finding the music pleasant to listen to, the people invited Tol-le-loo to come inside and continue playing. Soon all the people began to feel sleepy. Now Wit-tah-bah the Robin was pretty sure that Tol-le-loo was planning on stealing their fire, so he spread himself over the embers to protect it. And that is why the robin's breast is red today.

Meanwhile, Tol-le-loo kept playing his flute, and pretty soon everyone including Wit-tah-bah had fallen asleep. Seizing this opportunity, Tol-le-loo ran up to the sleeping Wit-tah-bah and cut a small hole in his wing. He then crawled through the hole and placed the fire inside his flute. He next ran out of the roundhouse and climbed to the top of Mount Diablo, where he built a great fire that lit up the entire country-side, including the blue mountains to the east where the Mountain People lived.

When Wek-wek awoke and saw the fire on Mount Diablo, he knew that Tol-le-loo had stolen the Valley People's fire. He immediately set out after Tol-le-loo, and eventually caught him. Tol-le-loo told Wek-wek to search him if Wek-wek thought he had the fire. Wek-wek searched but could not find the fire, because it was inside the flute. So Wek-wek tossed Tol-le-loo into the water and let him go.

Tol-le-loo got out of the water, and continued east to the mountains, all the while carrying the fire in his flute. Arriving home, he took the fire out of his flute, and placed it on the ground. Then covering it with leaves and pine needles, he wrapped it up in a small bundle. O-la-choo the Coyote smelled the fire, and wanted to steal it. He approached the bundle and pushed it with his nose, preparing to swallow it. Suddenly, the fire shot up into the sky and became the Sun. Le-che-che the Hummingbird and another bird went after it, but they could not catch it and returned without it.

The people took the fire that was left and put it into two trees, the buckeye and the incense cedar, where it still resides. That is why the Mountain People made their fire drills from the wood of these trees.

coming of the spanish—
and how diablo got its name

The first recorded sighting of Mt. Diablo by Europeans was by Don Pedro Fages in March 1772. The Fages expedition started in Monterey, moved up the coast of the East Bay and reached the Carquinez Straits; it is near present-day Antioch that Fages describes seeing Mt. Diablo. A second expedition in spring of 1776 was led by Don Juan Bautista de Anza, California's great colonizer. It reached the base of the mountain. Both Spaniards refer to the peak as "Cerro Alto [or Sierra] de los Bolbones [or Golgones]—meaning "Tall Hill [or Mountain] of the Volvon Indians." At that time most of the mountain lay within the homeland of the Volvons.

The first reference to "diablo" or "devil" in connection with the mountain derives from an incident sometime between 1803 and 1806 (accounts of the year differ). A small Spanish force came to the area in search of runaway mission Indians. The troops got as far as a settlement of the Chupcan people in a willow thicket near present-day Buchanan Field in Concord. They surrounded them, but the Chupcans slipped away during the night and crossed the Carquinez Straits to safety. The Spanish found it convenient to blame the devil for their embarrassment and called the place "Monte del Diablo," or "Thicket of the Devil." The area is designated Rancho Monte del Diablo in Mexico's land grant to Salvio Pacheco in 1834. Anglo settlers later mistook the word *monte* for *montana* ("mountain"), and fastened the name on the most obvious local landmark.

In his 1850 report to the state legislature, General Mariano Vallejo elaborated on elements of the story. He related that an "evil spirit"—"puy" in the aboriginal language, "diablo" in Spanish—had appeared on the side of the Indians, and helped them to disperse the Spanish sent to retrieve them. He also placed the incident at the foot of Mt. Diablo, confirming the mountain's connection with the name. In 1863 Bret Harte published a short story entitled "The Legend of Monte del Diablo," elaborating, in turn, on Vallejo's report. In this work of pure fiction (an adaptation of Christ's temptation in the desert) the devil appears to an 18th-century *padre* on the summit. There the priest is shown a vision of the future—the passing of Spanish California into American hands. The devil offers to detain the Yankee hordes on condition that the good father renounce his vocation. The offer is rejected and a fight ensues. Afterward the priest awakes, as from a dream.

By the mid-19th century, then, Diablo—Devil—was established as the mountain's name. There have always been those who have been offended by it, however. General Vallejo wanted the entire county to be named Diablo, but the state legislature, "after warm debates on the subject," resolved upon the "less profane" one of Contra Costa (the name by which the entire East Bay had once been known). In 1866 the state legislature, in response to a petition by members of the Congregational church, tried to change the name of the mountain to Coal Hill, but the town of Clayton resisted the attempt.

private ownership of mt. diablo and surroundings

The land on and around Mt. Diablo has changed hands innumerable times, but over the past 200 years the private uses of the land have largely stayed the same: cattle ranching, horse breeding, tourism, and mining have predominated.

After it acquired California in 1821, Mexico began handing out huge land grants to ex-soldiers and their families. In 1834, Dona Juana Sanchez de Pacheco was granted nearly four square leagues of land (approximately 17,000 acres), which included "Sierra de Golgones" (Mt. Diablo) and lands to the west. Approximately a quarter of her original rancho is now within park boundaries. It included Pine Canyon, Little Pine Canyon, the area surrounding the North Gate Road, and the Diablo and Turtle Rock Ranch inholdings. The Pacheco family used its land for grazing cattle but did not settle there. The Pacheco's Mexican land grant was confirmed by California in 1853.

The lands in the park were first surveyed between 1866 and 1875. The survey plats indicate that there was little early settlement within what is now the park boundaries, although a few settlers were established along the northern creeks (Mitchell, Back, Donner, and Diablo) by the 1870s. Green and Sycamore Valleys to the south of the park were also well populated.

Most public land within park boundaries was patented by the mid-1880s. A few small rancher-farmers owned land on the mountain, but by far the largest holdings were concentrated in the hands of two landowners, Charles McLaughlin and Seth Cook.

Charles McLaughlin was a railroad contractor and agent for the

Central Pacific Railroad. His holdings on Mount Diablo were part of a large land empire that he built up through his railroad dealings. In the vicinity of Mount Diablo McLaughlin owned the southern section of Mitchell Canyon, Deer Flat, White and Curry Canyons, and large tracts of land near the present park headquarters. He also held land in the Hidden Pond area. Most of this land was used for stock raising and grazing.

In 1873 William Cameron, one of the builders of the first toll road on the mountain, established a large estate in what is now the southern portion of the park. The estate went through rapid changes of management and ownership, all tied directly or indirectly to the Central Pacific Railroad. In 1877 David Colton, a business associate of the "Big Four," bought out the railroad's interests in the property. Between 1878 and 1912 the estate, known variously as Cook Farms and Oakwood Park Stock Farms, was enlarged by Colton's heirs, who raised stock and bred thoroughbred horses. By 1913 the estate included 15,000 acres and was considered the largest stock farm in the world, according to the Contra Costa News. It encompassed the areas of Dan Cook Canyon, Rock City, Devil's Slide, and the central portions of the park, along what is now the South Gate Road.

When Charles McLaughlin died in 1890, his land holdings were inherited by his daughter, Kate McLaughlin Dillon. Between 1890 and 1906 McLaughlin's daughter sold most of her father's holdings at Mt. Diablo. White Canyon and Deer Flat were purchased by Dominic Murchio, an Italian immigrant, who had previously established a ranch along Mitchell Creek north of the present park boundary. Over a period of eighty years the Murchio family added all of upper Mitchell Canyon to their ranch.

In 1912 Louise Boyd, Colton's niece, sold the Oakwood Park Stock Farm to a group of investor-developers led by Robert Burgess, a businessman born in Canada but raised in the Bay Area. Burgess was into land, lumber, ranching, and shipbuilding. He eventually owned much of the mountain, including the summit. He converted Oakwood Park Stock Farm—the former Cook estate—into Mt. Diablo Country Club. Between 1912 and 1915, he also built Mt. Diablo Scenic Boulevard. Like Joseph Hall's original toll roads, it was in two branches. One led from Ygnacio Valley in the west by way of Concord and Walnut Creek, the other originated in Danville.

All this was prelude to an elaborate scheme to create an exclusive residential park, and (again like Hall) build a great hotel and tavern on the mountain. The hotel was to be called Torre del Sol (Tower of the Sun), and William Randolph Hearst was to be one of its chief investors. Had Burgess' plans been realized, Mt. Diablo would be a very different place today. But the plan to build residential lots in the foothills foundered and Burgess filed for bankruptcy in 1917.

In 1928 W.P. Frick of Oakland bought much of the mountain, including the summit. Whatever development plans he may have had were forestalled when Californians passed a $6 million bond measure in 1930 for the creation of new state parks—including Mt. Diablo.

mining on the mountain

The most important minerals and rocks that have been mined or excavated on or around Mt. Diablo include mercury, diabase, graywacke, white sands, coal, blue schists, travertine, copper, and— farther north and east—gas and oil.

In 1863, copper ores with traces of **gold** were found on the slopes of Eagle Peak. This discovery set off a short-lived copper and gold rush on the mountain. No gold mining of any consequence resulted from these discoveries.

In 1863–64, **mercury** (quicksilver) was discovered on the northeast side of North Peak, and in Perkins Canyon. Mercury occurs in the form of cinnabar (red mercury sulfide) and metacinnabar (a black mercury sulfide). The host rock for ore is silica-carbonate rock, which is commonly spongy in appearance. A man named L. W. Hastings discovered cinnabar at what was later called the Rhyne Mine. The Rhyne Mine operated for about 10 years and briefly transformed Clayton into a roaring boomtown before becoming uneconomic. The Mine was open again between 1937 and 1947 when the war created a market for mercury. Twenty-four-hour operations resumed in 1951 under the Mt. Diablo Quicksilver Company, and continued until 1958 when prices again dropped. In 1933 black metacinnabar in the area known as the Mt. Diablo Mine was discovered and mined until the early 1970s.

It is estimated that about $1,500,000 worth of mercury was extracted from the mines. Mining was done from the surface, as well as from underground shafts. These operations ended up polluting Marsh Creek Reservoir, about 10 miles downstream from the old Rhyne Mine. The reservoir was closed to fishing in 1980 because its fish were discovered to have unsafe levels of mercury in their tissues. To this day, rain and the resultant water leaching through mining tailings from the operations will pollute Marsh Creek and the Marsh Creek Reservoir.

The **diabase** quarries on the north side of the mountain (Mt. Zion) yield gravel and riprap material. They are operated by Kaiser and RMC Pacific Materials. There were several excavations in **graywacke** on the north side of the mountain for the same purposes, but they are now abandoned. **Blue schist** from the Franciscan rocks on Mt. Diablo yielded good dimension stone and was popular for building construction due to its color.

A trivial amount of **copper** was produced from the mines in the diabase in 1863–1864; there is no activity now.

Travertine, a finely crystalline massive calcium carbonate deposit frequently associated with hot springs, was quarried along the north side of Mt. Diablo (Lime Ridge) for many years by the Cowell Cement Company.

North of Mt. Diablo and outside the park (in what is now Black Diamond Mines Regional Preserve), lignite **coal** beds in the Domengine Formation were for two decades the largest known and most extensively mined coal deposits in California. By the 1870s, mines in the towns of Somersville, Nortonville, Stewartville, West Hartley, and Judsonville (all northeast of Mt. Diablo) were producing more than 100,000 tons of coal a year. They fueled the rapidly expanding urban and industrial centers of the Bay Area. The last mine closed in 1902, as newer and cheaper energy sources became available. During their lifetime the mines produced approximately 4,000,000 tons of coal valued between $15 and $20 million.

At the base of the Domengine Formation exposed in the Black Diamond Mines Regional Preserve, there is a thin section of **white sands** called the 'Ione' sands, a description carried across the Central Valley from major white sand deposits in the Ione Formation on the east side of the Valley. The sands appear to be continuous across the valley subsurface and of equivalent age. The white sands that were used for making glass were mined from two deposits in the area from 1920 until 1949, when they ceased operation.

The Domengine Formation also acts as a reservoir for **natural gas** and the Martinez Formation produces **oil** in the subsurface northeast of Mt. Diablo.

mount diablo as a surveying axis

Mount Diablo served as a central point for three major 19th-century land and resource surveys: the survey of the public domain begun in 1851, the US Coast and Geodetic Surveys from 1852 to 1892, and the State Geological Survey in 1860–1864.

By the mid-nineteenth century, the national survey of lands had reached the West. Owing to its commanding position, Col. Leander Ransom, Deputy Surveyor General, chose Diablo as the base point to survey central California and western Nevada. On July 18, 1851, he and a crew of six established Mt. Diablo base (E–W) and meridian (N–S) lines by placing a flag at the summit. His report to the Surveyor General includes references to the heat of the day and the steepness of the terrain; one member of his team simply quit. Parcels of land in central California were long defined in terms of his survey, and deeds of sale were marked MDM—Mount Diablo Meridian. A brass monument marking Ransom's axis point is on view in the summit museum.

The US Coast and Geodetic Survey used Mount Diablo on several occasions as a base point for its national triangulation survey, undertaken to establish an accurate standard line as a base for future surveys and observations of the United States. Triangulation surveys were conducted at Mount Diablo in 1852, 1858, 1876, 1880, 1884, and 1892. The 1876 survey erected a signal station (a three-story structure) at the summit (which Joseph Hall later equipped with a telescope for the benefit of his Mountain House guests). Signals would flash to Mount St. Helena 50 miles away and to the Sierra Nevada 150 miles distant for the purposes of making height measurements. The station burned in 1891.

In 1860 the California Legislature appointed Josiah Whitney as State Geologist, charging him to make a complete geological survey of the state. The survey was to provide maps and full scientific descriptions of the state's rocks, fossils, soils, minerals, and botanical and zoological products. The actual fieldwork was conducted under the direction of William Brewer. In May 1862 the Geological Survey spent ten days at Mount Diablo, gathering fossils and botanical specimens, and measuring the mountain's height. Brewer praised the view from the top, saying "probably but few views in North America are more extensive—certainly nothing in Europe." Brewer also considered the mountain a key to many geological formations in the state. (See his journal *Up and Down California in 1860–1864.*)

mountain house hotel 1874–1895

Credit for building a hotel on the mountain belongs to Joseph S. Hall, a native of New Hampshire. He had earlier built a hotel on New Hampshire's Mt. Washington. In 1873 he was living in the San Ramon Valley and conceived a similar scheme for Mt. Diablo. He told

Mountain House. *Courtesy Contra Costa Historical Society.*

investors that Mt. Diablo "had more rare attractions to the lover of nature and fine mountain scenery than any mountain of the same altitude, perhaps in the world." He also promised that real estate values in the area would shoot up.

The first thing he needed was roads to the proposed site on the mountain. So on November 4, 1873 the Mount Diablo Summit Road Company was incorporated. Four months later, on February 18, 1874 the Green Valley and Mount Diablo Road Company was formed. The first financed a road, eight miles long, which traversed Ygnacio Valley through Pine Canyon to the top of Diablo. The second road, three miles long, ran from Danville through Green Valley. It intersected the other road at a point a mile from the summit.

Meanwhile, construction of the hotel got underway. It was called Mountain House, and was built where the two roads met. The roads and the hotel both opened in May 1874. Horse-drawn carriages ran twice-a-day service, stopping at the hotel. (Visitors who wanted to reach the summit could either hike the additional mile or go by horseback along the summit road.) During its first month of operation 800 people used the summit road.

Mountain House had sixteen rooms and for a time was very popular. Weddings, christenings, and like occasions were often celebrated there. Some people came and stayed for months. It was often said that no traveler had seen the west or California if he had not stayed at least one night in Mount Diablo's Mountain House to see the sun rise or set from the summit. In 1876, a three-story station was built at the summit as part of a government survey. Joseph Hall, who lived in the hotel along with his family, took the opportunity to install a telescope on top of the station, with seats all around. This made the hotel an even more popular destination.

The great naturalist John Muir describes a visit on December 5 1877 in a letter to his bride-to-be: "The sunrise was truly glorious. After lingering an hour or so, observing and feasting and making a few notes, I went down to that half-way hotel for breakfast. I was the only guest, while the family numbered four, well attired and intellectual looking persons, who for a time kept up a solemn, Quakerish silence which I tried in vain to break up. But at length all four began a hearty, spontaneous discussion upon the art of cat killing, solemnly and decently relating in turn all their experience in this delightful business in bygone time, embracing everything with grave fervor in the whole scale of cat, all the way up from sackfuls of purblind kittens to tigerish Toms. Then I knew that such knowledge was attainable only by intellectual New Englanders."

In July 1891 the great fire that burned much of the mountain's east side put the telescope out of commission. Whether owing to the fire, erroneous reports that it burnt the hotel also, or for other reasons, business at Mountain House tailed off in the 1890s. The hotel closed in 1895. The local ranchers, who had long objected to the existence of a hotel on Diablo and the stream of visitors across their land, successfully petitioned the board of supervisors to limit access to the roads as well. They argued that the tourists had caused the fire. Gates were installed, and for years it was necessary to get keys and permission from the ranchers to travel Hall's roads.

In 1901 the empty hotel burned to the ground. This time, it was the ranchers themselves who are thought to have been responsible. Tourists, especially students and teachers from UC Berkeley, were apparently still hiking to the hotel and summit, trespassing on the ranchers' land. In any case a ranch foreman, when charged with the burning, did not bother to deny it.

No trace of the hotel remains today. To visit its former site, follow the trail of the Old Stage Coach Road, located near the junction of North Gate and South Gate Roads. A more complete description of the site is given in the section on Short, Pleasant Hikes.

The Mountain House was a reality for only 20 years, but is still a highlight of Mt. Diablo's history.

beacon

In the late 1920s, the US Department of Commerce sponsored the creation of a network of beacon lights across the country to assist in night aviation. Mt. Diablo was chosen as the site for northern California. The WPA supplied the labor for the 75-ft. steel and concrete tower, Standard Oil paid for the materials. The company was partly fostering a market for its aviation fuel, much of it produced at their Richmond refinery (now Chevron). At the same time they got a chance to advertise their product by putting a large 'S' on the tower.

On April 25, 1928 Charles Lindbergh turned on the beacon by remote control from Denver. It had 10-million candlepower, rotated six times

The Standard–Diablo Beacon under snow. *Courtesy Contra Costa Historical Society.*

a minute (i.e. flashed every ten seconds), and was visible 100 miles away on a clear night. In 1939 the museum was built, and the beacon was removed to its top; the tower was disassembled. The beacon operated only two years more. After Pearl Harbor it was turned off for fear of another Japanese attack, this time on the west coast.

The beacon still crowns Mt. Diablo. It is turned on once a year, every December 7, to commemorate Pearl Harbor. The evening ceremony is open to the general public and is regularly attended by local veterans of Pearl Harbor, WWII, and other wars.

formation of a state park

In 1921, state senator Will Sharkey of Martinez successfully sponsored a bill in Sacramento declaring 630 acres on the summit of Mt. Diablo a State Park and Game Refuge. No money was attached to the bill. A park commission was appointed, and there was a ceremony on the summit June 19, 1921.

In 1927, Frederick Law Olmsted prepared a California Park Survey for the newly formed State Park Commission. Olmsted recommended acquisition of 5,000–6,000 acres at Mount Diablo to "amplify" and "round out" the small state park already located at the summit. Between 1931 and 1937 major properties were acquired along the route of the historic Mt. Diablo Scenic Boulevard, the North Gate Road, and at the summit.

Finally in 1930 Californians passed a $6 million bond measure that included money for Mount Diablo State Park. The park was officially dedicated on April 26, 1931 in the midst of rain, hail, and thunder.

During the 1930s the Civilian Conservation Corps did a great deal of work on Mount Diablo. They built and realigned the park roads, constructed hiking and fire trails, constructed ranger residences and maintenance buildings, developed campground and picnic facilities, in addition to building the Summit Building already discussed. The CCC work at Mount Diablo encompasses almost every type of project the CCC undertook in state and national parks. The facilities they built all belong to the style known as "rustic park architecture." It favors use of natural, unfinished, and—where possible—local materials, and achievement of an organic relationship between man-made structures and their natural surroundings. Examples of their work can be seen throughout the park but the most significant is undoubtedly the summit building, constructed in 1939–1942. The building is an octagonal tower built of rock quarried from the mountain itself.

Mount Diablo State Park grew very little between the late 1940s and 1965, when an ambitious acquisition program was initiated. As part of this program, several thousand acres have been added to the park, including the Macedo Ranch in Pine Canyon, the Murchio Ranch (Mitchell and White Canyons, and Deer Flat), the Devil's Slide area, Black Hawk Ridge, parts of Curry Canyon, the lower Alder Creek drainage, Meridian Ridge, and Donner and Perkins Canyons. Save Mount Diablo, a non-profit organization founded in 1971, played an active and important role in most of these acquisitions.

In 1965 the State of California acquired the Green Ranch, an inholding on the upper southeastern slope of Mount Diablo. In the mid-70s Save Mount Diablo negotiated for 2,052 acres to be dedicated to the park as a condition of the development of the Blackhawk residential community. Between 1966 and 1980 portions of the Diablo Ranch located in Pine Canyon were purchased by the State of California. In

1988 California voters approved a parks bond measure which gave the park $4 million to buy more land as Contra Costa population increased and open space decreased. The park now includes more than 19,000 acres; with city and regional open spaces and other public lands around the mountain, approximately 63,000 acres have been preserved.

KEY DATES IN THE HISTORY OF MOUNT DIABLO AND SURROUNDING OPEN SPACES

March 1772   **Fages–Crespi Expedition**   Lt. Pedro Fages and Father Juan Crespi explored along the Carquinez straits and skirted the western side of the mountain and down the San Ramon valley.

April 1776   **de Anza–Font Expedition**   Juan Bautista de Anza and Father Pedro Font, second expedition as far as the confluence of the Sacramento and San Joaquin rivers, and circling the northern part of the mountain from Pacheco to present day areas of Concord, Antioch, Oakley and Byron.

ca. 1805–1806   **The Naming of Mount Diablo**   The best sources suggest that Spanish soldiers in 1806 were pursuing native Americans as part of missionization, the natives took cover in a thicket (*monte*) near Pacheco, and the Spaniards camped with the intention of rounding them up in the morning. During the night the natives escaped across the Carquinez

Strait, an act only possible (according to the Spaniards) with the help of the devil (*diablo*). The thicket became known as Monte del Diablo; Anglo settlers later mistook *monte* for *montana* ('mountain'), and fastened the name on the most obvious local landmark.

July 31, 1834 **Rancho Arroyo de las Nueces y Bolbones** Rancho Miguel, normally known as Arroyo de las Nueces y Bolbones (or Golgones) Mexican land grant established for Dona Juana Sanchez de Pacheco, in recognition of the service of Corporal Miguel Pacheco 37 years earlier (confirmed 1853); included Pine Canyon, Little Pine Canyon and the Northgate Rd. area, Diablo and Turtle Rock Ranches, 17,734 or 17,782 acres (variously) including the "Sierra de Golgones" (derivative of "Bolbones"). Approx. ¼ of the land grant is within the State Park.

April 1850 **Naming of Mount Diablo** General Mariano Guadalupe Vallejo, in a Constitutional Convention report to the legislature, discussed the naming of Mount Diablo, with the intent of naming the County "Mount Diablo." "It was intended so to call the county [Mount Diablo], but both branches of the Legislature, after warm debates on the subject resolved upon the less profane [name] of Contra Costa."

1851 **Mt. Diablo Meridian and Survey** Colonel Leander Ransom, Deputy Surveyor General, established the initial point of the Mt. Diablo meridian at the mountain's summit, beginning the survey of public lands in California.

1859 **Mt. Diablo Coal Mines, Nortonville, Somersville, Black Diamond**   Coal discovered north of Clayton, and at Nortonville. The two towns ultimately included about 1,000 residents each. The soft, high-sulfur coal was eventually superseded by higher quality coal from Oregon and Washington, and out-competed by coal carried by the transcontinental railroad completed in 1869. Somersville and Nortonville mines closed around 1885, Nortonville briefly reopened in 1932.

April 30, 1862 **Geological Survey of Mt. Diablo, Description of View**   Josiah Whitney, William Brewer and the State Geological Survey return to near Mt. Diablo to camp by the mountain on Tuesday, May 6 and to ascend the mountain on Wed., May 7. Brewer writes: "The view was one never to be forgotten. It had nothing of grandeur in it, save the almost unlimited extent of the field of view. The air was clear to the horizon on every side, and although the mountain is only 3,890 [actually 3,849] feet high, from the peculiar figure of the country probably but few views in North America are more extensive—certainly nothing in Europe… Rising from the great plain, and forming the horizon for three hundred miles in extent, possibly more, were the snowy crests of the Sierra Nevada. What a grand sight! The peaks of that mighty chain glittering in the purest white under the bright sun, their icy crests seeming a fitting helmet for their black and furrowed sides! ...I had carried up a barometer, but I could scarcely observe it, so enchanting and enrapturing was the scene."

1863–4   **Mercury, Rhyne Mine**   L.W. Hastings discovered quicksilver (mercury) on the northeast side of North Peak and Perkins Canyon, mined until the 1950s.

1865–66   **Legislative Attempt to Change the Name of Mt. Diablo**   The state legislature made an unsuccessful attempt to change the name of Mount Diablo to "Coal Hill."

1873   **First Wagon Road up Mt. Diablo, Hall, Mountain House Hotel**   Green Valley and "Mount Diablo Summit Road Company" incorporated. First wagon road up the mountain, two roads constructed by local investors including William Cameron and Joseph Seavey Hall, who also built the 16-room Mountain House Hotel a mile below the summit (2,500 foot elevation, operated through the 1880s, abandoned 1895, burned c. 1901). In 1876 the US Coast and Geodetic Survey erected a 3-story signal station at the summit, which was later equipped with a telescope by Joseph Hall for use of Mountain Home guests. (Signal station burned 7/4/1891, when fire swept up from Morgan Territory.)

mid-1880s   **Land Ownership at Mt. Diablo State Park**   Most
public land in present day state park area patented,
largest landowners include Charles McLaughlin (railroad contractor and agent for Central Pacific
Railroad) and Seth Cook.

1912   **Mount Diablo Development Co.**   Louise Boyd,
David Colton's niece, sold Oakwood Park Stock Farm
to R.N. Burgess and his Mount Diablo Development
Co., a group of investors, (10,000 acres, $150,000
($15/acre), who wanted to create an exclusive resi-
dential park, remodeled Cook's Clubhouse/Casino
as the Mt. Diablo Country Club (he was Club presi-
dent from 1912–1919), and opened Mt. Diablo to
the public (they won out over S.F.'s Olympic Club).
He subsequently acquired the area later known as
Blackhawk ranch and all the land between it and
Diablo, up to the summit, including the Mt. Diablo
Base Meridian Monument and the right-of-way to
Mt. Diablo Scenic Boulevard. The golf course was
designed by Jack Nevelle, who later designed Pebble
Beach.

1912–16   **Mt. Diablo Auto Toll Road**   Burgess' group built
a new toll road (North Gate and Mt. Diablo Scenic
Boulevard—completed 1915), accessible to auto
traffic. Burgess' Mount Diablo Development Co.
planned tower-hotel "Torre de Sol", never built, visited by William Randolph Hearst summer, 1916,
with the hope of financing and national publicity.
The deal called for Hearst to buy 15,000 acres at

$1000/acre from the Ygnacio Valley to the top of Diablo and down its southeast slope.

1917   **Interest in Diablo Development Waned,** both from the public and from W.R. Hearst; the contract was never signed, although there had been substantial publicity including the automobile races held from Oakland to the top of the mountain. R.N. Burgess resigned from the Mt. Diablo Country Club and filed for bankruptcy.

1921   **Mt. Diablo State Park Created**   Mt. Diablo was one of seven state parks created before the establishment of the California State Park System in 1927, a "state park and game refuge" on 630 acres (from Burgess' Mount Diablo Development Co.), administered by its own appointive Mount Diablo State Park Commission.

1927–28   **California Park Survey**   Frederick Law Olmstead prepared a statewide California Park Survey (the Olmstead Plan) for the newly created State Park Commission, recommending acquisition of 5–6000 acres to "amplify" and "round out" the small state park at the summit. Major properties were acquired along the historic Mt. Diablo Scenic Boulevard (South Gate Rd.), the North Gate Road, and at the summit.

1928   **Standard–Diablo Tower**   Standard Oil of California constructed a 75-foot aviation beacon, the

Standard–Diablo (SD) tower, jointly with the U.S. Dept. of Commerce to encourage, and as a guide for, commercial aviation. Visible for 100 miles, first lit by Charles Lindbergh, later transferred to Summit Building and now lit only on Dec. 7, Pearl Harbor Day.

1930s **CCC Era on Mt. Diablo** Civilian Conservation Corps (National Park Service administered, men ages 18–28, paid $30/month plus room and board) constructed Camp Diablo on the Danville side of Mt. Diablo and built facilities at Mt. Diablo (among the best in the State's parks), realigning park roads, hiking and fire trails, residences, picnic areas and campgrounds, dams, and the Summit Building, in style known as "rustic park architecture," emphasizing natural appearance, local materials, organic relationship between structures and surroundings.

1939–42 **Summit Building Constructed** with rock from Fossil Ridge quarry; planning begun in 1934, approved 1939, completed 1942.

Dec. 7, 1971 **Save Mount Diablo Founded** jointly by Art Bonwell and Dr. Mary Leo Bowerman. SMD was created because the subdivisions were spreading toward the mountain, and no organization was working primarily on the area.

1974 **Blackhawk Ranch** Ken Behring acquired 4200 acres of the Ranch from Howard Peterson, who had decided to sell when the county reassessed the land as a potential subdivision. The Blackhawk subdivision was proposed in 1973, prior to the sale. Save Mount Diablo negotiated for 2,052 acres to be dedicated to Mount Diablo State Park as a condition of development, including much of the Blackhills–Wall Point area, Blackhawk Ridge, parts of Dan Cook and Jackass Canyons, and the area below Oyster Point, the single largest donation ever to MDSP.

1974   **Mount Diablo Interpretive Association** founded as a nonprofit organization to assist the state in conserving, developing, and interpreting the Park for the benefit of the public.

1988   California voters approve a **bond measure** which gives the park $4 million to buy more park land.

1993   **Summit Museum and Visitor Center** dedicated.

1999   **Mitchell Canyon Interpretive Center** opened by Mt. Diablo Interpretive Association working with Mt. Diablo State Park.

2002   Mount Diablo State Park has grown to about 19,000 acres.

animals of the park

Mt. Diablo is home to many animals and a preserve for much of the wildlife that originally dwelt in the surrounding area.

The **cougar** (or **mountain lion**) does occur on the mountain, but it would not be entirely accurate to say that there is a mountain lion population on Mount Diablo. Lions have been known to range over 20 miles in one night. They use Mount Diablo as part of their range. Cougars require so much territory that the park will be only part of it, and only one or two cats may be in the area at any one time.

The **bobcat** is the size of a medium-small dog; it is recognizable by the white tuft of hair on its elevated hindquarters. Although common in the park, it is extremely shy and not often seen. Bobcats eat rodents, rabbits, birds, and the occasional deer.

The **grey fox** is widespread and abundant on Mt. Diablo; park residents often spy them at night along park roads. Foxes eat rodents, insects, and berries.

The **coyote** is also common, especially in the rolling hills at lower elevations; it may often be heard from at night. Coyotes eat mainly rodents and carrion. Despite their reputation, they rarely attack livestock; many of

Bobcat. *Courtesy Michael Sewell/Visual Pursuit.*

the livestock kills blamed on coyotes are actually caused by dogs, then scavenged by coyotes. Coyotes will feed on any dead animals they find.

Blacktailed deer are often seen in the morning or evening or when there are few park visitors. As its name suggests, Deer Flat is a good place to look. Deer are browsers, feeding on grass, shrubs, herbs and acorns. They are preyed upon by mountain lions, bobcats, sometimes coyotes.

Rabbits feed on grasses, herbs, and shrubs. They are an important food source for bobcats, foxes, coyotes, and eagles. There are two true rabbits on the mountain, the cottontail and the brush rabbit; they are similar in appearance. The jackrabbit is actually a hare, and can be identified by its longer ears and legs.

Feral pigs have become a serious problem in the park. They "rototill" the ground, uprooting vegetation and causing erosion. They will eat anything, including endangered species like the Alameda whipsnake. They are thought to descend from farm pigs that escaped. Pigs may be spotted in clusters near streams or other water sources.

Grey Fox. *Courtesy Michael Sewell/Visual Pursuit.*

Coyote. *Courtesy Margo Watson.*

The burrows of the **botta pocket gopher** can be found throughout Mt. Diablo. Gophers feed on roots, grasses, herbs, and seeds.

Two squirrels inhabit the park. The **California ground squirrel** is extremely common in developed areas, where ground cover has been artificially reduced. They are absent from much of the backcountry, partly because of the extensive eradication program conducted by the county in the park up until 1974. The **fox squirrel** is the common red-brown squirrel seen on trees and power lines throughout the Bay Area.

Raccoons are found throughout the park, especially around water and developed areas. They frequently steal food from park visitors and get into garbage cans. (Please do not feed them.) Their natural diet includes frogs, berries, insects, reptiles, eggs, and small mammals.

Domestic cattle have been grazed on Mt. Diablo since the 1800s.

Grazing is permitted in a restricted section of the park, as part of the park's policy of preserving some of the region's traditional land use. The ranch is called the Interpretive Working Cattle Ranch and is a 1000-acre section in the Macedo Ranch area.

The most common variety of **rattlesnake** on the mountain is the northern Pacific (*Crotalus viridis oreganus*), a sub-species of the western rattlesnake (*Crotalus viridis*). The northern Pacific rattlesnake is dark gray, olive, yellowish brown, brown, or black, and has dark hexagonal or circular blotches with light borders. The average length ranges from 1½ to 2½ feet with the maximum length being just over 5 feet. They eat small rodents, birds, and lizards, and live for 16–20 years. They are preyed upon by hawks, eagles, coyotes, and bobcats —and by man, who kills them out of fear or ignorance. Although rattlesnakes can be aggressive when hungry or threatened, they do not often bite humans. A bite with venom (the snake does not always inject venom when it bites) can cause swelling, necrosis, fever, and nausea. The only way to treat a bite is to get to a hospital within four hours and receive anti-shock and anti-venom treatment.

Rattlesnakes hibernate throughout the winter, though they may emerge briefly on a warm winter day. The females generally give birth every two years although it can vary from every year to every third year. The gestation period is 110 days and they give birth to an average of 10 live young. Mt. Diablo abounds in the snake's main requirement, adequate hiding spots, such as ground squirrel burrows or rocky outcroppings. Although shy and elusive, they can sometimes be spotted crossing park trails or roads.

The **Alameda whipsnake** is sooty black with yellow-orange stripes running the length of its body. It can grow to 4 feet and within its range is found most often on Mt. Diablo. It eats lizards, rattlesnakes, small mammals, and birds. The snake is known for its speed, which it will use to retreat from humans. In 1997 the Alameda whipsnake was added to the federal government's list of threatened species. The action by the U.S. Fish and Wildlife Service means the snake is eligible for federal habitat protection and restoration funding.

From August through October is **tarantula** time on Mt. Diablo. During this turn of the season park visitors often see the hairy arachnids slowly making their way across roads and trails.

The tarantula spends most of its life in and around its underground burrow. But when a male tarantula reaches maturity at around seven years of age he leaves the safety of his subterranean home to risk life and (all eight) limbs in search of a mate. These males are the autumnal wanderers we see on the mountain.

Once a female tarantula is located by scent and enticed out of her den by tapping, the male tarantula faces the problem common to all male spiders: he must convince the female he is a suitor and not just lunch. Toward this end, male tarantulas have small spurs or hooks on their

front legs to hold the female's savage jaws at bay while they mate.

A male that survives mating and is not killed by the female still faces a bleak future. He never returns to his borrow and will die at the onset of cold weather. The female, for her part, will

Threatened Alameda whipsnake.
Courtesy Michael Sewell/Visual Pursuit.

return to her burrow and go on mating, ultimately to hatch hundreds of baby spiders the next spring. Female tarantulas live up to 25 years.

The tarantula is North America's largest spider. But despite its fierce appearance, it is mild-mannered and fairly innocuous. Its bite is no more severe than a bee sting. The spider's preferred defense mechanism is to flick the top of its abdomen with its rear legs. This action directs a spray of barbed hairs into the nasal passages and mucous membranes of any small mammal bent on making the tarantula its next meal. This behavior is why a tarantula will frequently have a bald spot on its abdomen.

Tarantula. *Courtesy Michael Sewell/ Visual Pursuit.*

This hair-flicking defense is ineffective against the tarantula's most feared enemy, the tarantula hawk wasp. This wasp seeks out and attacks the tarantula. After delivering a paralyzing sting, the wasp drags the tarantula to a hole and lays its eggs on the helpless creature. When the eggs hatch, the young wasps eat the tarantula alive. Tarantula wasps can frequently be found in stands of anise. To locate tarantula burrows, look for a hole in the ground about the size of a quarter and covered by a web. (The larger, funnel-shaped webs numerous at lower elevations are made by funnel spiders, not tarantulas.)

birds

Mount Diablo provides birders with a large public area in which to explore birds of several habitats (including chaparral, oak woodlands, grassland and rocky outcrops). Over two hundred bird species have been sighted on the mountain, and it is well known to birders for its superb examples of chaparral birds, spring migrants, numerous raptors, and such locally elusive species as Prairie Falcon, Hermit Warbler, Hammond's Flycatcher, Calliope Hummingbird, Sage Sparrow, and Black-chinned Sparrow.

Birds can be sighted year round, but spring is one of the most exciting times: April and May for migrating and singing species, June for breeding/nesting species.

BIRDING LOCATIONS:

In general, the majority of good birding is in the canyons and the lower half of the mountain. Probably the three finest areas for birding are Pine Canyon, Mitchell Canyon, and the Rock City area. The best examples of chaparral birds can be found in the area from just below Toyon Picnic area to Pioneer Horse Camp and also around Muir Picnic Area. The canyon areas such as Dan Cook Canyon and Curry Canyon can provide some shade in the heat of summer but avoid these two sites in winter. The area from Curry Point to Knobcone Point has the driest trail in rainy weather (and one of the hottest temperatures in summer). All of the canyons can be terribly muddy during the rainy season. Mitchell and White Canyon can be very exciting in April and May and is one of the least demanding of the trails. Donner Canyon can be equally exciting during this same time, but it is very rugged as are most of the areas around the peaks (such as Eagle and North Peaks).

The Summit area is generally poor birding, although during spring migration one can sometimes see Black-chinned Sparrow, Hermit Warbler (sometimes common), Calliope Hummingbird, Lawrence's Goldfinch (probably regular here in late spring) and (rarely) Cassin's Finch. Blue Oak and Oak Knoll picnic areas can be superb in May, especially for warbler flocks. If on a short driving tour of the mountain in spring, start at South Gate Road and check the areas of Rock City, Curry Point area, Junction Campground area, Wildcat Group Camp, and Blue Oak–Oak Knoll picnic areas and, if time permits, a few pull-outs along North Gate Road (especially for Lark Sparrow, Rufous-Crowned Sparrow, Rock Wren and Golden Eagle).

PINE CANYON

Pine Canyon is located on the southwestern side of Mount Diablo. It has numerous access points, each having their own merit. Two favorite access points are Macedo Ranch parking lot (at the very north end of Green Valley Road out of Danville, self-registration parking here for two dollars) and the Castle Rock Road parking area for Diablo Foothills Regional Park and the private Castle Rock Park (free public parking just outside the kiosk for Castle Rock Park out of Walnut Creek. The public trail goes around the edge of Castle Rock Park; access through Castle Rock Park is uncertain but usually permitted if you don't linger here). It is also possible to access this area from Burma Road (at North Gate Road 3 miles up from the kiosk; this is rather short but steep and has virtually no shade) or from the Barbeque Terrace–Wildcat Group Camp area of South Gate Road (a longer hike and furthest from the best birding sections).

No matter what direction you access Pine Canyon, the best birding is the Pine Pond area and much of the lower half of the canyon. This canyon can have miserable footing from December through at least

March in rainy weather—numerous stream crossings, plus much of the soil here is clay. At present Pine Creek flows down the main fire road near Pine Pond during the winter creating a real mess (plus the overflow from Pine Pond bisects the trail). Also a word of warning: rattlesnakes are regular in this canyon, especially by Pine Pond. The canyon can be crowded on weekends. Regular birds in the general area include Golden Eagle, Canyon Wren (difficult to actually see), Rock Wren (especially by Sulphur spring area, the rocky area above Macedo Ranch called "China Wall," and a rocky area in the upper part of the canyon), Brown Creeper, Lawrence's Goldfinch, Redshouldered Hawk, Cooper's Hawk, Willow Flycatcher (mainly mid-August through September at Pine Pond), Rufous-crowned Sparrow, Lark Sparrow, Varied Thrush, White-throated Swift (mainly morning and evening), White-tailed Kite (mainly near Barbeque Terrace), Cassin's Vireo, Chipping Sparrow, Lazuli Bunting, Hairy Woodpecker, Hammond's Flycatcher (mainly in April and early May), Bullock's Oriole, Black-headed Grosbeak, Ash-throated Flycatcher, Western Kingbird, etc.

Pine Pond and the adjacent forest is often a magnet to birds. Over 150 species have been sighted within a half-mile of the pond. Pine Pond has been slowly filling in over the years and seems to have fewer rarities every year, but is often the only chance of finding waterbirds in the park. Some of the birds to be found by Pine Pond include Wild Turkey, Spotted Sandpiper, Blackcrowned Night-Heron, Green Heron, Virginia Rail, Sora, Piedbilled Grebe, Bufflehead, Ring-necked Duck, Wood Duck, Cinnamon Teal, Green-winged Teal, American Wigeon, White-throated Sparrow, Barn Owl, Lincoln's Sparrow, Yellow-breasted Chat, MacGillivray's Warbler, Sage Sparrow (out of their normal habitat here—probably post-breeding birds), Lewis's Woodpecker, etc. Many of these birds are rather rare here.

MITCHELL AND WHITE CANYON

Mitchell and White Canyon are mainly accessed from Mitchell Canyon Road in Clayton. This canyon is by far the easiest canyon to bird by foot. The trail can be muddy in winter and is heavily used on weekends (watch out for speeding bicyclists, ticks, and rattlesnakes). Mitchell Canyon generally lacks the water birds of Pine Canyon—although there is a small pond between Mitchell and Donner Canyon—but has more chaparral birds. In late April to mid-May these canyons can sometimes have a massive warbler fallout (including MacGillivray's and Hermit). Hammond's Flycatcher seems to be a regular migrant here in spring. White Canyon (and sometimes middle to upper Mitchell Canyon) is by far the best site in the park for Calliope Hummingbird, mainly from late April to mid-May. Black-chinned Sparrow is sometimes seen here, and Sage Sparrow is regular. Phainopepla has been seen at Deer Flat and elsewhere in the canyon (also check just outside of the park along Mitchell Canyon Road in winter and spring). Lawrence's Goldfinch is regular here in spring during some years.

chaparral birds

Mt. Diablo's extensive and relatively easy accessible chaparral provides an unequaled opportunity for birdwatchers to explore its mysteries. Chaparral birds are notorious for being shy, however, and can be difficult to view. Observers should take advantage of their use of conspicuous singing perches and should familiarize themselves with their vocalizations. Sometimes an individual shrub (such as Toyon) can be loaded with ripe berries and will attract a large variety of birds. Many of the chaparral birds are actually very curious and can be easily attracted by a practice known as "squeaking." This is a series of assorted noises made by the birdwatcher, the principal one being a slurred call that resembles the admonishment "shhh." Note, though, that birds are easily frightened by sudden movements. Birds in breeding season are also more easily disturbed by white than by colored clothing.

Extensive chaparral is located along Wall Ridge (accessible from either Rock City or Macedo Ranch) and along Knobcone Point trail (access from Curry Point). A very productive area along Summit Road is the section from the Pines Picnic Area to Pioneer Horse Camp. Muir Picnic Area is productive nearly year-round. White Canyon is often visited by birders, although it has rather dense chaparral and it can be difficult to view chaparral birds here.

Species include:

California Quail (year-round)
Anna's Hummingbird (year-round)
Western Scrub Jay (year-round)
Bushtit (year-round)
Canyon Wren (year-round where boulders or caves are present)
Bewick's Wren (year-round)
Wrentit (year-round)
California Thrasher (year-round)
Spotted Towhee (year-round)
California Towhee (year-round)
Rufous-crowned Sparrow (year-round)
Sage Sparrow (year-round)
Common Poorwill (year-round, but mostly April to August; nocturnal)
Ash-throated Flycatcher (April to September; needs at least a few
    trees)

Blue-gray Gnatcatcher (mostly March to October)
Orange-crowned Warbler (mostly February to September)
Lazuli Bunting (April to September)
Black-chinned Sparrow (mostly late April to June)

In winter, look for the permanent residents plus:
Sharp-shinned Hawk (commonly hunts over chaparral)
Townsend's Solitaire (rare)
Hermit Thrush
American Robin (mainly around Toyon bushes)
Varied Thrush (uncommon)
Fox Sparrow (often the most abundant species)
Golden-crowned Sparrow (common)
Dark-eyed Junco (a permanent resident, but more common here in
    the winter)
Purple Finch

During migration also look for:
Calliope Hummingbird (rare)
Rufous Hummingbird
Yellow Warbler
Townsend's Warbler
Hermit Warbler (mostly in May)
Lawrence's Goldfinch (nearly year-round, but mostly seen in spring)

Chaparral birds are not uniformly distributed, with many species
showing marked preferences for certain microhabitats. Sage and
Black-chinned Sparrow strongly prefer burned-over chamise or where
there are gaps in the chamise. Rufous-crowned Sparrow usually
prefers California Sagebrush or Poison Oak clumps. Old stands of

Acorn woodpecker

Black phoebe

Chestnut-backed chickadee

Northern Mockingbird. *All photos this page courtesy of Brian Murphy.*

Plain titmouse

pure chamise or pure stands of Coyote Brush usually have the least interesting birdlife. Burned areas usually become very productive about 3 years after a fire. The Wall Ridge area, site of recent fires, is good for birding for this reason.

The most sought after bird in the park by visiting birders is probably the **Black-chinned Sparrow**. It is best found by looking for singing males in the morning from mid-May to mid-June, probably peaking soon after Memorial Day weekend. Its preferred habitat is burned-over areas of chaparral (or stunted chaparral with large gaps) that are dominated by chamise that is more than two years, but less than twenty years old. Some years the species is fairly common and in other years it is nearly absent. In recent years, the best sites have been along Fossil Ridge (hike out of Uplands Picnic Area through the gap in the grassland), South Gate Road at about two-tenths of a mile below South Gate kiosk (also park at Uplands Picnic Area and hike back down the road as there is no parking below Rock City), the area around Pioneer Horse Camp to Blue Oak Picnic Area, and Muir Picnic Area. Birds (mostly far from the trail) can also be had at Wall Ridge (excellent habitat at present), Mitchell Canyon, the south side of the Fire Interpretive Trail, Prospector's Gap Road, Juniper Campground, and at various burn sites along lower South Gate Road.

The **Peregrine Falcon** population began shrinking in the 1950s throughout the U.S. owing to widespread use of DDT. By the 1970s, they were nearly extinct. In the spring of 1989, two baby peregrines were re-introduced to the park in a program led by Save Mount Diablo in co-operation with the Lindsay Wildlife Museum. They were placed with prairie falcons, and watched over to make sure they were accepted. There is now a stable population of peregrines in the park. They usually migrate to the coast in the winter, but return to Mt.

Peregrine Falcon. *Courtesy Michael Sewell/Visual Pursuit.*

Diablo in the spring. They can be identified by their distinctive dive, which they use to hunt or defend their territory, and which can reach 200 miles an hour. By virtue of this behavior, they are accounted the world's fastest bird. They can be seen using this tactic to defend their territory against other raptors such as Red-tailed Hawk.

A bird checklist for Mount Diablo is available from Mount Diablo Interpretive Association or from the State Park.

other fauna

Seventy species of **butterfly** are known to occur on Mount Diablo, almost 50% of all known species in the San Francisco Bay Area. When looking for butterflies, choose a sunny day with a temperature of 55° or higher (usually between 10am and 3pm). Very few butterflies fly when it is cool, foggy or rainy. A pair of binoculars is very useful, especially those that can focus 10' or closer. (Note that collecting butterflies is prohibited.)

For locating butterflies, there is no other single nectar source locally better than the long white blossoms of the California buckeye. It blooms from about the first week in May to the third week in June, differing greatly from site to site. The nectar of this plant may be different from other plants, for the butterflies at these blossoms are unnaturally tame. (The nectar may have an intoxicating or narcotic effect, as it is poisonous to bees.)

Other good nectar plants in spring for butterflies on Mount Diablo include yerba santa (perhaps the next best species after California buckeye), coyote mint (excellent), narrow-leaved goldenbush, yarrow, and Oregon sunshine (*Eriophylium lanatum*). In the higher parts of Mount Diablo, where California buckeye is rarely found, these plants can be particularly productive when searching for butterflies (especially for a number of rarer species).

Variable checker-spot butterfly.
Courtesy Liede-Marie Haitsma.

At lower and middle elevations butterflies sometime seek nectar in spring at Brodiaea and its allies, lupines, milk thistle (excellent) various yellow mustards (especially winter cress) and mule fat (*Baccharis viminea*). In summer and fall some of the best nectar sources include the blossoms of toyon, narrow-leaved milkweed (excellent), bull thistle (excellent), yellow star thistle, hedge mustard, nude buckwheat and gum plant (*Grindelia camporum*).

Observing buckeye trees on sunny days in Pine, Mitchell, Donner, Curry, and Dan Cook Canyon can be very productive. Binoculars are often necessary for seeing the butterflies (especially the hairstreaks) at the tops of these trees. The common (chalcedon) checkerspot is often the most numerous butterfly on these blossoms. Sometimes up to 200 individuals can be found on a single large tree. Other species you might encounter on the California buckeye in the Mount Diablo area include: Mourning Cloak, Red Admiral, Lorquin's Admiral, California Sister, Northern Checkerspot, Editha Checkerspot, California Tortoiseshell, West Coast Lady, Painted Lady, Buckeye, Satyr Angle-wing (more common at Las Trampas Wilderness), Callippe Fritillary, Monarch, California Ringlet, Cabbage Butterfly, Alfalfa Butterfly, Large Marble, Great Copper, Echo Blue, and Acmon Blue, Goldhunter's Hairstreak, Hedgerow Hairstreak, Dryope Hairstreak, Great Purple Hairstreak, California Hairstreak, the Farmer, Umber Skipper, Mourn-ful Duskywing, Propertius Dusky-wing, Anise Swallowtail, Pale Swallowtail, Western Tiger Swallowtail, Two-tailed Swallowtail, Pipevine Swallowtail (more common at Las Trampas), etc.

Female butterflies often can be found if one knows the host plant for its eggs. For some butterflies, such as the small-veined (mustard) white, the season is very short (spring only). It seems to prefer milk-maids as both its host plant and as a nectar source.

Pipevine Swallowtail is rare away from its only host plant, Dutchman's pipe (*Aristolochia californica*). In the Mount Diablo area this plant is probably only found at Diablo Foothills Regional Park. Callippe Fritillary's only host plants are violets, and it is somewhat restricted to their range.

Male butterflies of many species can be encountered at either hilltops or at moist areas. "Hilltopping" and "puddling" in male butterflies appears to be related to breeding activities. Swallowtails provide the classic example of male hilltopping butterflies defending their territory. The summit of Mount Diablo is a good place to see the male Pale Swallowtail and Two-tailed Swallowtail. Puddling in butterflies is very widespread and usually involves newly hatched males.

There are several species of **ladybug** in California, the most prominent of which on Mt. Diablo is *Hippodamia convergens*. Most winters these colorful insects appear on the mountain by the hundreds of thousands. Guided by some inner map, they mass in the same sheltered ravines, dispersing in the spring to search for food. Look for swarms of adult ladybugs in dark, shaded ravines, especially on the Falls Trail.

Mitchell Creek has traditionally supported a small remnant population of **rainbow trout** thought to be native. They were the only remaining wild trout in the creeks that drain into Walnut Creek. In 1985, 13 were captured during inventory of a 240-ft. section; based on this sample, 190 fish were estimated to be there overall. But surveys performed in 1997 found none. Efforts are currently underway to determine whether any trout survive in Mitchell Creek, and, if they do, to restore the canyon to a healthier state for their benefit.

trees and flowers

Mt. Diablo has an unusual variety of plant communities because of three factors: the range in elevation; the diversity of soil types (owing to the mountain's complex geology); and the fact that the mountain is in a transition zone, sharing climate characteristics with both the cool coast and hot Central Valley.

The mountain is also transitional in that it represents the northern limit of some plant species (e.g. black sage and Coulter pine), the southern limit of others (e.g. Hooker's onion). And it has several endemic species—plants found here and no place else. They are:

Mt. Diablo manzanita (*Arctostaphylos auriculata*)

Mt. Diablo sunflower (*Helianthella castanea*)

Mt. Diablo globe tulip (or globe lily) (*Calochortus pulchellus*)

Mt. Diablo bird's beak (*Cordylanthus nidularius*)

Mt. Diablo phacelia (*Phacelia phacelioides*)

Mt. Diablo jewel flower (*Streptanthus hispidus*)

Six major wildlife-biotic communities on the mountain can be identified: riparian woodland, grassland, chaparral, foothill woodland (oak savannah), marsh/vernal pool areas, and rocky outcrop/cliff areas.

riparian

Riparian vegetation occurs along the banks of permanent streams. Sometimes the surface water is absent in the summer, but the water table remains near the surface. Tree roots sink down to a shallow, permanent water table and thus are able to compensate for the long summer drought. Typically the vegetation is mixed woodland containing broad-leafed winter-deciduous trees such as bigleaf maple *(Acer macrophyllum)*, willow *(Salix spp.)*, sycamore *(Platanus racemosa)*, California black walnut *(Juglans hindsii)*, flowering ash *(Fraxinus latifolia)*, white alder *(Alnus rhombifolia)*, Fremont cottonwood *(Populus fremontii)*, buckeye *(Aesculus californica)*, and California bay *(Umbellularia californica)*.

On Diablo, riparian communities are found in the canyons. The better-watered among them are distinguished by the frequent presence of alder, sycamore, and cottonwood. Mitchell and Donner Canyons have permanent streams. In Donner Canyon, Fremont cottonwood is rare and confined to the lower part. At its lower end Curry Canyon is broad and open. Large trees of sycamore and, toward the mouth, Fremont cottonwood, grow on the floor. Alder is absent. During the summer the water table is twenty feet below the surface. The lower part of Alamo Canyon contains a permanent stream fed by a spring in the streambed. Alder and bigleaf maple predominate along the stream, with some sycamore. Pine Canyon is dry and without true riparian species.

The town of Walnut Creek is named for the black walnut, and is probably one of its original homes. Although the nut is very tasty, the shell is so hard to remove that it is not a viable crop. The hulls, however, produce a useful dark brown dye. The white alder is a tall, graceful tree that is never far from water. They are leafless in winter and regain their leaves soon after the blossoms appear. Fremont cottonwoods are named for the masses of cottony hairs attached to their seeds. Spring in Mitchell Canyon often brings great masses of these seeds covering the ground like so much snow.

Riparian woodlands have several stratified zones relating to the frequency and duration of flooding, and distance from the stream course. Nearest the water is an almost bare strip, frequently scoured by water. Above this is a shrub-dominated area of willows. Their branches and roots trap sediments. Higher on the banks is a layered canopy dominated by Fremont cottonwood affiliated with maple, sycamore, white alder, black walnut, California bay, and willow. Below these tall trees are tangled layers of shorter trees and shrubs, including box elder *(Acer megundo)*, blue elderberry *(Sambucus cerulea)*, hazelnut *(Corylus cornuta* var. *californica)*, coyote bush *(Baccharis pilularis)*, and poison oak *(Toxicodendron diversilobum)*. Abundant, too, are climbing vines such as honeysuckle *(Lonicera hispidula* var. *vacillans)*, blackberries *(Rubus vitifolius)*, currants *(Ribes* spp.), California grape *(Vitus californica)*, Dutchman's pipe *(Aristolochia californica)*, clematis (virgin's bower) *(Clematis ligusticifolia)*, and wild cucumber *(Marah fabaceus)*. Where there is sufficient light smaller plants are found including wild rose, scarlet monkeyflower *(Mimulus cardinalis)*, sticky monkeyflower *(Mimulus guttatus)*, California nettle *(Utica californica)*, snowberry *(Symphoricarpos rivularis)*, and common horsetail *(Equisetum arvense)*.

Riparian vegetation creates a diversity of wildlife habitat. Fish and amphibians thrive along sheltered stream banks, and many birds and mammals feed, breed, and migrate within the layered overstory.

grasslands

Today the native grasslands of Mt. Diablo are gone. In fact, relatively few of California's grasslands and open places have been untouched by humans. Many were quite different communities that were altered deliberately or accidentally, in many cases by removal of shrubs and trees. Such open places are "disturbed"—meaning there is little natural vegetation. Plowing, tilling, grazing, and burning have so altered the original vegetation that few native plants have survived.

The original grassland communities were dominated by perennial, native bunchgrasses —grasses that grow in a clump from the ground and that go dormant and turn brown in summer but do not die. Some live for 30 years. Such grasses as purple needle grass (*Stipa pulchra*), nut grass *(Cyperus* sp.*)*, and squirreltail *(Sitaniion)* are representative of the original flora. Hundreds of different kinds of annual, perennial,

Bunchgrass, perennial. *Courtesy Bob Walker/IDG Films.*

and bulb-bearing wildflowers also occur between bunchgrasses, providing a display of ever-changing color from March through early June. Only a few such areas in California remain to remind us of the splendor of these original grasslands.

About fifty species of grass grow in the park, and about half are introduced. These exotic (non-native) species are mostly annuals. Annuals live only one year, beginning growth after winter rains. They reproduce by seeds alone, dying during the summer drought. All parts of the plant die, leaving no underground part for propagation. This is an advantage because the seed is drought-resistant, long-lasting, easily transported, and will germinate whenever the climate allows. The most common plants now are annuals introduced from Europe. Wild oat *(Avena fatua)* is the most widespread. There is also soft chess *(Bromus mollis)*, foxtail *(Hordeum jubatum)*, filaree *(Erodium* sp.*)*, California bur-clover *(Medicago polymorpha)*, Italian rye *(Lolium perenne)*, bromes *(bromus* spp.), and fescue *(Festuca* spp.). Some of these alien grasses and flowers were brought in by design, others were introduced by accident—often as contaminants of crop seeds (wild oats with cultivated oats, for example); as useful hay crops (alfalfa; sweet clover; red clover), as food plants (cardoon, chicory, fennel), or in ballast or bricks.

Meanwhile, flowers with weedy characteristics and long-range dispersal strategies began to fill the spaces between grasses. The greater the grazing pressure, the more the "armed" weeds like cardoons and thistles took over. Today, much rangeland has been degraded by pernicious, spiny weeds, especially yellow star thistle. This lacks prickly leaves, but the bright yellow flower heads are surrounded by radiating spines. A near relative, the purple star thistle, is well armed with prickly spines on the leaves as well.

One exception to our grassland story is grasslands on serpentine soils. Serpentine rock—California's slick, soft, shiny bluish-green rock of metamorphic origin—is notorious for its barren, nutrient-poor soils. Serpentine soils are low in essential calcium, high in toxic heavy metals such as molybdenum and nickel, and overly rich in magnesium, a needed nutrient that is nonetheless toxic in large quantities. Consequently, only certain specialized native flowers and grasses evolving over the eons have managed to adapt to serpentine soils. Alien weeds and grasses are unable to grow here, so serpentine grasslands give us fine examples of bunchgrasslands in their near-original state. On Diablo there is a band of serpentine with its characteristic vegetation that runs east–west through Murchio Gap extending west along Long Ridge.

Since 1992 there has been an effort on the part of volunteers to restore native grasslands to selected areas in the park, especially around Mitchell Canyon. Indigenous species have been planted, and controlled burns have been conducted to clear the area and foster growth of perennials, whose root system can survive a burn to put out new leaves in the spring.

Myriad species of wildflowers, including annuals, summer-dormant perennials, and bulbs, light up the grasslands in spring after the winter rains. Some years the non-native grasses get a head start, and wildflowers end up stunted; other years, wildflowers begin growth with or before the grasses and appear in vividly colored masses. Some of the most common include owl's clover *(Orthocarpus densiflora)*, buttercup *(Raniculus californica)*, shooting star *(Dodecatheon hendersonii)*, California poppy *(Eschscholzia californica)*, popcornflower *(Plagiobothrys nothofulvus)*, blue dicks *(Dichelostemma capitatum)*, Mariposa lily *(Calochortus venustus)*, fiddleneck *(Amsinckia intermedia)*, and vetch *(Vicia* spp.*)*. Wildflowers come in many shapes and sizes, but most are white, blue, purple, or yellow: "bee" colors. (Bee eyes do not perceive orange and red.). Bees are the most abundant, prolific pollinators of open space.

chaparral

The word "chaparral" comes from Spanish *chaparro*, meaning "scrub oak." In California, however, the term is applied to plant communities of dense, evergreen shrubs and, taxonomically, these shrubs are mostly not oaks. Chaparral is found on hotter, drier, slopes, such as those adjacent to South Gate Road and Summit Road. It is also the dominant community on the ridges around Twin Peaks and North Peak. From a distance the dense, tall shrubberies of chaparral look like uniform dark green baize draped over the mountainsides. A good place to see chaparral species up close, as well as experience their cumulative effect from a distance, is on the Meridian Ridge trail on the mountain's north side.

Characteristic chaparral species are: chamise *(Adenostoma fascicula-tum)*, with tiny, needlelike leaves; black sage *(Salvia melifera)*, with dark-green, aromatic leaves; yerba santa *(Eriodictyon californicum)*, with shiny, dark-green leaves; coyote bush *(Baccharis pilularis)*, an aggressive pioneer; toyon (California holly or Christmas berry—*Heteromeles arbutifolia)*, coffee berry *(Rhamnus californica)*, with dark purple berries; mountain mahogany *(Cercocarpus betuloides)*, with grayish bark and serrated leaves; California lilac *(Ceanothus* spp.), with thick, shiny leaves; and various species of manzanita *(Arctostaphylos* spp.*)*, with smooth, red bark, pale green leathery leaves, and urn-shaped flowers. Also present are scrub oak *(Quercus* *dumosa)* and poison oak *(Toxicodendron diversilobum).*

Of all the chaparral shrubs on Mt. Diablo, chamise (shah-MEES) is the most widespread, often found in pure stands on the driest, rockiest slopes. It is readily identified by its tiny, narrow leaves that turn oily and shiny on hot days (giving it its alternative name, "greasewood"). In late May to early June the shrubs are transformed by spirelike clusters of creamy-white flowers, each resembling a single, minute rose. Manzanitas exhibit great variety, from low, creeping shrubs to near-trees up to twenty feet tall. But all have smooth, red-purple bark; simple, untoothed, ovate, leathery evergreen leaves, and clusters of small, urn-shaped white or pink flowers in the winter or early spring. The Mt. Diablo manzanita *(Arctostaphylos auriculata)* is endemic to the mountain; it has softly felted, gray, clasping leaves and pink flowers.

Botanists distinguish between "hard chaparral" shrubs—so called because they have stiff, tough, durable leaves that are seldom shed even at the peak of summer's heat; and "soft chaparral": small shrubs with soft leaves that are often heavily scented — smelling of sage, turpentine, or mint — which helps keep animals from browsing them. Among hard chaparral shrubs, leaf design varies as much as the several families and general species represented. Manzanitas make stiff ovate leaves that are turned edgewise or vertically to avoid the full brunt of sun—and some kinds, like big-berry manzanita *(Arctostaphylos glauca)*, have whitish leaves that reflect away excess light and heat. Chamise *(Adenostoma fasiculatum)* uses narrow, needlelike leaves clustered together to conserve water by minimizing surface area exposed to the sun. Wild lilacs (ceanothuses) cover their leaves with a thick, waxy covering that makes them shiny. Bush poppy *(Dendromecan rigida)* has bluish green leaves held obliquely to reflect away heat and minimize the impact of the fierce summer sun.

Soft chaparral shrubs are varied, with some particularly aggressive pioneer species, such as coyote bush (*Baccharis pilularis*). Others include California sagebrush (*Artemisia californica*), with broad dark green leaves whose edges curl under; sticky monkeyflower (*Diplacus aurantiacus*), with sticky, viscid green lace-shaped leaves, again with curled-under edges; black sage (*Salvia millifera*), with highly aromatic dark green, narrowly triangular leaves; blue witch (*Solanum umbelliferum*), a green-twigged shrub whose fuzzy, light green leaves are cast away in summer; and poison oak (*Toxicodendron diversilobum*), with shiny, tripartite leaves, which are lost early during severe drought.

In addition to their ingeniously designed leaves, chaparral shrubs have deeply probing roots that serve to hold shrubs in place and find sources of deeply hidden water. Chaparral is a drought-tolerant landscape cover.

Most chaparral shrubs have a similar growing period, but flowering in the community may extend over a period of six months or longer. Manzanitas typically flower in midwinter or very early spring and produce vegetative growth after flowering. In contrast, chamise produces vegetative growth in late winter or early spring and then flowers in June. Toyon also blooms in June and July. Ceanothus flowers in April when soil moisture is optimal and air and soil temperature are warming.

Typically, chaparral vegetation is a single layer of impenetrable shrubs four to eight feet tall, with intricately branched, interlacing canopies. The ground is bare of plants, soils are shallow and stony, and the surface is covered with dry litter. For these reasons, chaparral is prone to burning and many chaparral species show an ecological adaptation to repeated burnings, called "crown sprouting." In these shrubs, the above-ground portion of the plant may be destroyed by hot brush fires, yet the plant still produces numerous new shoots that develop from a large burl at the top of the root system at or below the soil surface. As a result, crown-sprouting shrubs re-establish quickly after a fire and do not go through a period of seedling establishment.

Chaparral shrubs grow into nearly impenetrable canopies—from head high to well over ten feet tall. The best way to pass through is to crawl beneath the branch canopy as small mammals do. Chaparral has been called the "elfin forest" in consideration of this dense but short, forestlike growth pattern.

oak savannah

Many different oak species are found on Mt. Diablo. Coast live oak *(Quercus agrifolia),* interior live oak *(Q. wislizenii),* canyon live oak *(Q. chrysolepis)* California black oak *(Q. kelloggii),* blue oak *(Q. douglasii)*, and valley oak (*Q. lobata)* are all represented. Oak woodlands have thirty to sixty percent tree cover and more than sixty trees per acre. Sometimes trees are crowded together, but the canopy cover is still open enough to support grasslands beneath.

The live oaks (coast live, interior live, and canyon live oak) are evergreen. They do not drop their leaves in the fall. The leaves tend to be small, tough, spiny, and have a leathery texture that prevents them from wilting. They are also rich in tannins and chemicals offensive to herbivores, and conduct photosynthesis at a low rate. Such leaves are "sclerophyllous" (hard-leafed). This prevents loss of moisture.

Coast live oak is one of the most common trees on Mt. Diablo. Native

Americans favored the acorns as a food source, grinding them into meal. Bedrock mortar pits can still be seen on the margin of (appropriately named) Live Oak Camp. Coast live oak tends to favor the moistest places and is therefore more abundant on the south side of the mountain and in canyon bottoms. Interior live oak tends to favor the driest places and is therefore more abundant on the northern and eastern sides of the mountain. Canyon live oak is somewhat intermediate in terms of moisture requirements, with the finest stand at Juniper Camp.

Deciduous oaks (black, blue, and valley oak) turn brown and drop their leaves in autumn, have bare branches in winter, and produce new foliage in spring. Their leaves are lobed in the fashion of many eastern oaks. Deciduous oaks do not live exclusively apart from live oaks; the two types often intermingle. Valley oaks are the most majestic of the deciduous oaks, with branches dropping so low they almost

Valley Oak (Quercus lobata). *Courtesy Liede-Marie Haitsma.*

touch the ground. Mature trees may be more than 200 years old. They are most common at the base of the mountain, often growing alone on grassy flatlands. Blue oaks are much smaller and spindly. They are easily recognizable by the bluish-green cast of their leaves, and by their leaves' shallow lobes. Black oaks, the least common on Mt. Diablo, favor steep, north facing slopes in the Lower Rock City area. They are common in Morgan Territory, east of Mt. Diablo.

All oaks are prone to tumor-like growths up to three inches in diameter, commonly called "oak apples." These are insect-formed plant galls. Tiny, dark wasps, from the family of wasps called the "cynipids" feed on plant tissues and produce a substance that stimulates the tree into making these galls; galls are actually plant growth. A tiny wasp egg becomes encased in the gall providing both food and a living chamber for the larvae. In summer the pupa turns into an adult and chews its way out of the gall. The wasps are tiny, harmless to people, and cause no serious permanent injury to the tree. More than 100 different kinds of galls are found on oaks, which form on leaves, buds, twigs, branches, roots, and even the acorns. Each cynipid wasp species forms a gall of a particular size, shape, and color. Jumping oak galls are common under valley oaks. Other galls on blue oak are cone shaped, or round and fuzzy, or shaped like tiny loaves of bread. Although they only harbor wasps once, galls often remain on the tree long afterward, turning dark brown and becoming spongy with age. Native Americans used them for kindling.

All oaks, but weakened ones especially, may be infected by parasitic flowering plants called mistletoe. Mistletoe is easiest to spot in winter on deciduous oaks, when it may be the only spot of green in an otherwise bare tree. Instead of soil, mistletoes grow from branches, where they penetrate the bark to obtain water and nutrients.

All oaks produce acorns, though these differ greatly in size and shape (see accompanying table for Diablo's species). Many different kinds of animals, from insects to rodents, depend on acorns for food. They were originally a staple of the Native American population on Diablo too, though they have to be ground and leached to be palatable for human consumption. They are then made into mush or bread.

Alongside blue oak and interior live oak one often finds California buckeye *(Aesculus californica),* Foothill (gray) pine *(Pinus sabiniana)* and Coulter pine *(Pinus coulteri)*. Both Coulter and Foothill (gray) pine have gray-green foliage and very large cones. They are sometimes called the big-cone pines. Coulter pine has the biggest, heaviest cone of any native conifer species—up to a foot long and weighing several pounds. Both species are drought adapted, growing on exposed mineral soils with poor water retention. Foothill (gray) pines have sparsely clustered, drooping needles, resulting in a "see-through" appearance. Also distinctive are their multiple trunks, which may diverge near the base. Coulter pines have thicker, bushier needle clusters. There are good stands of Coulter pine in Mitchell and Back Canyon.

Oak woodlands are also home to the Mt. Diablo fairy lantern *(Calochortus pulchellus),* otherwise known as Mt. Diablo globe tulip. This lemon yellow flower is endemic to Mt. Diablo (grows only on Mt. Diablo) in shady spots on north-facing slopes. It blooms in April and May and can be found in Mitchell Canyon, around Rock City, and other areas between 700 and 2,500 feet in elevation.

KEY TO THE TREE OAKS OF MT. DIABLO

I. Leaves lobed, deciduous (falling in winter or during severe drought), thin and supple.

> a. Leaves small (1–3 inches long) and shallowly lobed or with wavy margins, green or (esp. in later summer–fall) bluish-green, and falling from twigs by winter. Acorns oval and up to 1½ inches long. Bark light gray or whitish. Conspicuous in lower Donner and Mitchell Canyons.
> **Blue oak** *(Quercus douglasii)*

> b. Leaves large, three to six inches long, deeply lobed, with a soft bristle on each sharply pointed apex. Acorns oblong and from 1 to 1½ inches long. Bark rough and blackish, especially on older specimens.
> **California black oak** *(Q. kelloggii)*

> c. Leaves small (2–4 inches long), with 7–11 deep, rounded lobes. Acorns conical, 1 to 2 inches in length. Bark light gray or whitish, gray and deeply furrowed on mature trees. The largest western oak—sometimes called Weeping Oak because of its pendulous twigs. There are many prominent specimens in and around Deer Flat.
> **Valley oak** *(Q. lobata)*

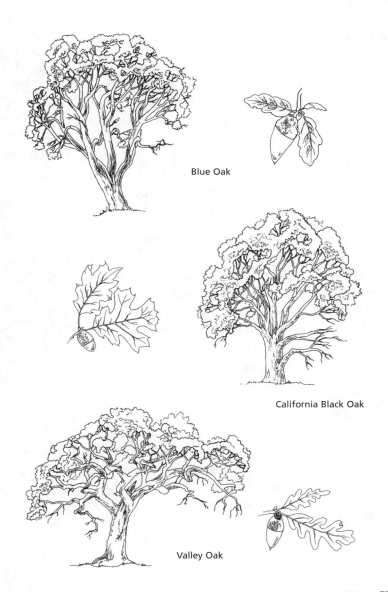

Blue Oak

California Black Oak

Valley Oak

II. Leaves never lobed, evergreen, usually thick and stiff.

a. Leaves flat, elliptical, and only 1 to 2 inches long; margins may be smooth or toothed; upper surface dark green and shiny, lower surface similar or slightly yellow-green. Acorns narrow and conical, up to 1½ inches long. Bark smooth and dark, becoming fissured with age. The tree is usually as broad as it is tall, with numerous horizontal branches that parallel or intersect the ground. Favors the dry northern and eastern sides of the mountain.

Interior live oak *(Q. wislizenii)*

b. Leaves flat and elliptical, 1 to 2½ inches long; margins smooth or toothed, often alternating on the same tree; upper surface dark green and shiny, lower surface pale blue-green, often with a thick coat of golden or gray hairs, and with 6–10 pairs of mostly parallel veins. Broad-based acorns are 1 to 2 inches long. Bark on mature trees whitish or light gray and smooth. Large community at Juniper Camp and common elsewhere.

Canyon live oak *(Q. chrysolepis)*

c. Leaves wide and convex, from 1 to 4 inches long, with spiny margins. Conical acorns from ½ to 1½ inches in length, with a rich, reddish-brown color. Bark smooth and dark on the outside, reddish inside, with shallow furrows on older specimens.

Coast live oak *(Q. agrifolia)*

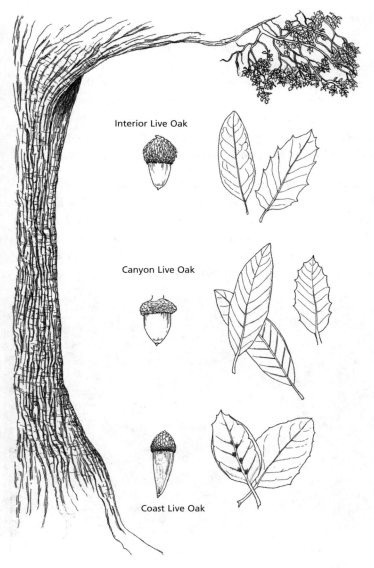

Interior Live Oak

Canyon Live Oak

Coast Live Oak

springs and ponds

Mount Diablo is home to dozens of springs, primarily on the south side of the mountain. Springs and seeps occur where the water table intersects the surface. This results in a marshy area with associated vegetation that requires year-round moisture and is often highly rare or specialized. Characteristic species are California sunflower *(Helianthus californicus)*, Indian hemp *(Apocynum cannabinum)*, durango root *(Datisca glomerata)*, and various knotweeds *(Polygonum* spp.*)*.

The south side of the mountain also hosts several ponds, often in association with springs. Frog Pond lies in a natural hollow just below the chaparral west of Rhine Canyon, at an altitude of 1550 feet. Hidden Pond is a permanent pond that lies in a secluded natural hollow on the flat east of Mountain Springs Canyon, just below the chaparral at an altitude of 1700 feet. Chase Pond is a shallow, vernal

Donner Creek, Clayton Open Space. *Courtesy Bob Walker/© IDG Films.*

(vernal meaning "spring"—i.e. it dries up in the summer) pool near the saddle south of Mountain Springs Canyon at an altitude of 1800 feet. Sheepherders' Pond is a small winter seasonal pool on the south side of the peak 300 yards east of the meridian, at an altitude of 1600 feet. Characteristic plants include sedges *(Carex* spp.), spreading or common rush *(Juncus patens)*, cattails *(Typha latifolia)*, and various reeds *(Scirpus* spp.). Nearly all the plants are perennials with shallow root systems and a tall grasslike appearance.

rocky outcrops

Rocky outcrops, rock faces, and scree slopes support highly specialized vegetation—mostly annuals or low-growing woody perennials. Eagle Peak, North Peak, and the Fire Interpretive Trail near the summit are characteristic locations of the largest outcrops. On the south side of Mt. Diablo there are a series of chert outcrops extending from the summit to the margin of the chaparral one thousand feet lower. Large outcrops occur in Rhine Canyon and on the adjacent ridges. On the north side of the peak the outcrops are numerous but generally smaller.

Elsewhere, exposed rock faces are scattered within grassland, oak woodland, and chaparral communities. Characteristic species include juniper *(Juniperus californica)*, mountain mahogany *(Cercocarpus betuloides)*, scrub oak *(Quercus berberidifolia)*, red rock penstemon *(Kecjuekka corymbosa)*, California fuchsia *(Zauschneria californicum)*, birdsfoot *(Lotus* spp.*)*, sticky monkeyflower *(Mimulus aurantiacus)*, coffee fern *(Pellaea andromedaefolia)*, bitterroot *(Lewisia rediviva)*, Brewer's rock cress *(Arabis breweri)*, and various buckwheats *(Eriogonum* spp.*)*.

early spring wildflowers of mount diablo

The winter rains and increasing daylight of early spring trigger a spring bloom for many of Mount Diablo's native wildflowers. The exact timing and quantity of blooming wildflowers will vary greatly year to year as it is controlled by a number of environmental factors. By late February there are a number of flowers to view, especially in the chaparral and at low-elevation grassy hilltops. The following include most of the more striking species that one might find in the first three months of the calendar year.

Bear brush *(Garrya fremontii)* starts off the new year in a bizarre manner by blooming in early January at the summit of Mount Diablo. This uncommon evergreen shrub, resembling the evergreen oaks in both leaf and flower, produces two-inch-long pale lavender catkins on the male shrubs. Blooming may be triggered by the increasing daylight as it often blooms in icy conditions. The more common coast silk-tassel *(Garrya elliptica)* is easily found between Curry Point and Sycamore Canyon in February and March.

Manzanita *(Arctostaphylos* sp.) is perhaps the star attraction of December to March. These evergreen shrubs with red bark fill the chaparral (and a few wooded slopes) with delicate white to pink tiny bell-like flowers that attract a great number of insects and the occasional hummingbird. The Mount Diablo manzanita *(Arctostaphylos auriculata)* grows only around Mount Diablo and has the pinkest blossoms of the mountain's manzanita. It is easily seen around Wall Ridge, Live Oak Campground and also between Curry and Knobcone Point.

Another early bloomer is chaparral currant *(Ribes malvaceum).* This deciduous shrub often begins blooming in late December at lower elevations, finishing at the summit around early May. The flowers are pink and quite striking when seen in mass. It is easily seen around Knobcone Point and along Summit Road. The similar gooseberry (*Ribes* sp.) differs in having thorns and smaller flowers. Mitchell Canyon and the summit area are good places to look for it.

Indian warrior *(Pedicularis densiflora)* is a semi-parasitic herbaceous plant of chaparral–pine areas. The red-green leaves are a pleasant sight in early March along Wall Ridge or Curry to Knobcone Point. It blooms in April at the summit. The newly opened leaves are pure red in this and many other species as a protection against ultraviolet light.

Members of the mustard family are well-known early bloomers. Milkmaid *(Cardamine californica)* is very common just about every-where on Mount Diablo, often occurring in heavily shaded forests. Its simple white flowers can be common by mid-February at low elevations, finishing at the Fire Interpretive Trail in May.

California's state flower, the California poppy *(Eschscholzia californica)* blooms nearly year round, mostly March to October on Mount Diablo. Its lacy gray-green leaves and golden yellow to orange flowers are well known to most Californians. It is generally found in the grasslands below 3500 feet. Check North Gate Road in mid-April to early May for peak mass bloom.

Buck brush *(Ceanothus cuneatus)* is an evergreen shrub that is fire dependent, as it gets crowded out in older stands of chaparral. Its mass of white blossoms (smelling like popcorn) starts in early February along lower South Gate Road, finishing in May at the Fire Interpretive Trail. Jim brush *(Ceanothus oliganthus)* is another of the

Fuchsia

Wild Mustard

Owl's Clover

California Poppy

Red Western Columbine

Woolly Paintbrush. *All flower photos courtesy Jan Briggs.*

Baby Blue Eyes

Woolly Mule's Ears

Blue-eyed Grass

California Fuchsia

Chinese Houses

Hound's Tongue

Lupine

Mt. Diablo Globe Tulip

Mt. Diablo Sunflower

Wild Pansy

Wind Poppy

Birds Eye Gilia

so-called California lilacs. It has powder-blue blossoms and blooms from late March through May, more commonly on the north side of the mountain.

Very pleasing to the eye in early March is Johnny-jump-up *(Viola pedunculata)*. These are golden yellow with black markings and have a striking reddish-brown underside. Look for it at Curry Point. Much smaller and more widespread on the mountain is the similar-looking mountain violet *(Viola purpurea)*, blooming March to May. It is fairly common in the area around the summit.

Brewer's rock cress *(Arabis breweri)* is found on rock outcrops at 1200 feet to the summit. Its small pale-green leaves grow in rock crevices and it has beautiful pink to purple flowers (that later form curved seedpods). The summit area is the best site to study this species, but also look for it at the Falls Trail in Donner Canyon.

Mosquito-bill *(Dodecatheon hendersonii)* is the common species of shooting star around Mount Diablo. The nodding pink flowers are quite adorable, especially when in mass. The leaves are simple and basal. Look for it from mid-February through April, especially in Mitchell Canyon where it is very common.

Grand hound's-tongue *(Cynoglossum grande)* is a widespread member of the forget-me-not family on Mount Diablo, most found in wooded areas of light shade. It has foot-tall flower stalks with powder-blue to violet flowers. It usually is well in bloom by March 1 at lower elevations, and finishes in late April along the Fire Interpretive Trail.

geology

Our understanding of the geological history of the rocks and structure of Mt. Diablo has undergone major changes during the past 30 years, and even now geologists are still trying to unravel the complicated history of the mountain. This complex history is not unique to the mountain, but to our region as a whole, since Mt. Diablo has been caught up in the processes that have shaped the Coast Ranges over the past several million years.

Perhaps the most salient fact is that, although the rocks of which it is composed are very old, Mt. Diablo only began rising recently in geological terms. The rocks are old, the mountain itself is young.

the rocks of mount diablo— their type and history

To better understand the complex geology of Mt. Diablo, it is useful to divide the mountain's rocks into three main groups. Each group has a different history and is characterized by different types of rocks.

Group 1—Mt. Diablo Ophiolite (*Mesozoic*)

Group 2—Franciscan Assemblage (*Mesozoic*)

Group 3—Great Valley Group (*Mesozoic*) and
Younger Sedimentary rocks (*Cenozoic*)

Plate tectonics played a major part in the formation of the Mesozoic rocks of Mt. Diablo. We now recognize at least 11 separate major plates of oceanic crust and rigid upper mantle rocks around the globe. These plates "float" on a layer of semi-molten rock, all moving against and jostling each other, creating new land forms in the process. Continents ride atop these ocean plates, being rafted along as the plates move. New ocean crust is being continually created by the eruption of submarine volcanic material forming along ocean-spreading ridges such as the Mid-Atlantic Ridge. To compensate for the newly created oceanic crust, older existing ocean crust is driven beneath the continental crust at "subduction zones," and recycled into the earth.

GROUP 1—MT. DIABLO OPHIOLITE (*MESOZOIC*)

It is generally believed that near the close of the Jurassic, a subduction zone existed in the Sierra foothills. At that time, subduction jumped to a zone along the coast of present-day California. The ocean crust caught between these two zones was preserved and later partially exposed. The exposure of this old ocean crust on Mt. Diablo has been named the Mt. Diablo Ophiolite. *Ophiolite* refers to ocean crust found on land. The Mt. Diablo Ophiolite underlies the mountain north of a line drawn from Long Ridge through Murchio Gap, encompassing the Zion Peak rock quarry, Mitchell Rock, and Eagle Peak. [*See Figure 2.*]

Radiometric and fossil-age determinations date the ophiolite as having been formed at an oceanic spreading ridge approximately 169 million years ago during the mid-Jurassic. Based on the age of overlying continentally derived sediments, one can infer that this part of the ocean crust arrived at the continental edge in late Jurassic, perhaps from as far west as 5000 miles.

Mt. Diablo Ophiolite Basalt: The ophiolite is an igneous rock solidified from sub-marine lava flows. The basalt making up a part of the Mt. Diablo Ophiolite is mainly interbedded *pillow basalts* and *basalt*

geological time scale–mount diablo
(times in millions of years)

era	period	mya	epoch	
CENOZOIC	**QUATERNARY**	.01	Recent (Holocene)	Recent Alluvium
		1.6	Pleistocene	Livermore Gravels
	TERTIARY	5.3	Pliocene	Tassajara Formation
			Miocene	Green Valley or Sycamore Formation (*includes Blackhawk Quarry Horizon*)
				Neroly Formation
				Briones Formation (*includes Cierbo Formation*)
		24		"Monterey"
		37	Oligocene	Kirker Formation
		57	Eocene	Domengine Formation
		66	Paleocene	
MESOZOIC	**CRETACEOUS** 66 144			Great Valley Group / Franciscan Complex / Ophiolite
	JURASSIC 208			
	TRIASSIC 245			

Figure 1.

flows. As the basaltic lava erupts under water, the outer surface of the flow "freezes" in contact with the water. More lava breaks through and again the outer surface "freezes." This process leads to the accumulation of "pillow" structures and the resultant rock is referred to as *pillow basalt.* The basalt has a microscopic crystalline texture with a black to greenish-brown color, weathering to a yellowish-brown to dark reddish-brown soil. Well-developed pillows can be seen on Mitchell Rock.

Mt. Diablo Diabase: The pillow lavas are fed by a series of vertical fissures, or *dikes,* that allow the molten rock from below to reach the surface. The molten material in the dikes solidifies into a rock called *diabase,* which has the same chemical composition as basalt, but with a coarser texture. Diabase is exposed in quarries at Mt. Zion and on Eagle Peak.

Mt. Diablo Serpentine: Serpentine is a rock frequently found in association with an ophiolite. *Serpentine* is derived from the basal portion of the original ocean crust and uppermost part of the mantle, but has been metamorphosed by hydration from ocean water circulating through fractures in the ocean crust. The new minerals formed are commonly the serpentine minerals antigorite, chrysolite, and lizardite. Serpentine, incidentally, is California's state rock.

On Mt. Diablo, serpentine occurs in several localities. The largest is the prominent east-west band that runs through Murchio Gap extending west along Long Ridge, separating the ophiolite on the north from the Franciscan rocks exposed in the central core of the mountain to the south. This band is characterized by a noticeable change in vegetation due to the high magnesium content of the serpentine. Exposures of the serpentine are typically pale green to greenish-gray, locally black, weathering to grayish-orange.

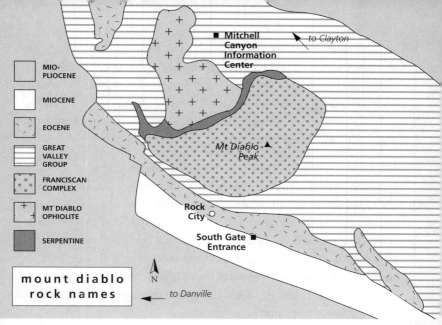

Figure 2.

GROUP 2—FRANCISCAN COMPLEX (*MESOZOIC*)

The central Mt. Diablo summit area and North Peak is underlain
by an assemblage of Mesozoic rocks that have been a puzzle to
California geologists for years. Our relatively new understanding of
plate tectonics and subduction has finally provided an important clue
to unraveling this mystery. This diverse complex of rock types is common up and down the coastal ranges of California and has been given
the name Franciscan Complex or Assemblage. The mixing of such a
wide variety of rock materials can be accounted for by the processes
of subduction.

The Franciscan Complex records over 140 million years of uninter-
rupted east-dipping subduction, during which the Franciscan formed

as an accretionary complex. As the oceanic plate subducted beneath the continent, part of the upper section of the ocean crust (pillow basalt) and the material riding on the plate (chert, graywacke, shale, small islands, and sea mounts) were scraped off the upper part of the subducting plate, mixed together, partially subducted and accreted on and under the continental crust.

Mt. Diablo and North Peak are composed of faulted blocks of resistant basalt and chert with some graywacke and minor shale, and are expressed topographically as rugged and jagged rock masses. Wrapping around the two peaks in a rough "figure 8" shape are the more gentle treeless slopes of "melange." The Franciscan "melange" is essentially a chaotic mixture of an intensely sheared sandstone and shale "paste" in which are embedded blocks of basalt, chert, and graywacke along with rare exotic rocks. It is often difficult to distinguish between the melange topography and local landslides.

Franciscan basalt: The blocks of basalt exposed in the Franciscan on Mt. Diablo are altered oceanic pillow basalt. On the surface the rock weathers to a dark yellowish-brown to dark reddish-brown while fresh exposures are grayish-green to light olive drab. It is locally called "greenstone." The green color comes mostly from chlorite, a green alteration mineral. The basalt blocks in the Franciscan are believed to be fragments scraped off of the upper part of subducting basaltic ocean crust.

Franciscan chert: The chert bodies in the Franciscan form prominent dark red exposures and talus slopes. Made up of silica, they are resistant to erosion and form such features as Devil's Pulpit and Turtle Rock. Typically red in color (green and white less common), the chert layers are typically interbedded with reddish-colored shale. The banded rocks are often referred to as "ribbon chert." The red color is derived from iron oxides.

The chert in the Franciscan was formed far out at sea. Silica skeletons of minute ocean animals called *radiolaria* settled to the ocean floor forming a silica ooze that ultimately solidified into chert. The chert continued to slowly accumulate on top of the ocean floor as the ocean crust drifted away from the spreading center on its long journey toward subduction. The chert ranges in age from 190 myo (million years old) to 90 myo, representing 100 million years of accumulation.

Franciscan graywacke: Graywacke is less common on Mt. Diablo than the greenstone and chert. It is typically fine- to medium-grained and massive (no stratification or bedding visible). It breaks along distinct jointing planes, which helps distinguish it in outcrop from the more "shatter fracturing" of the greenstone. It is a fine- to medium-grained sandstone consisting mainly of angular quartz, plagioclase feldspar, chert fragments, and dark volcanic rock fragments. Calcite and quartz occur commonly in the criss-crossed white veins.

The graywacke is younger in age than the greenstone (basalt) or chert, ranging from 90 to 100 million years in age. These rocks are thought to have formed in a subduction trench environment off the coast of North America (some researchers suggest Mexico, subsequently moving north). The degree of metamorphism of the graywacke indicates burial to at least a depth of 15 miles before uplift and exposure.

Franciscan shale: Approximately 10% of the Franciscan on Mt. Diablo is made up of shale. Most of this clay-sized material was probably deposited in less turbulent current conditions in association with the graywacke deposition.

Franciscan exotic rocks: The most common exotic rock present on Mt. Diablo is a glaucophane schist, or "blue schist," named for the noticeable blue color of the glaucophane. Blue schist is largely altered basalt and reflects a history of hi-pressure/low-temperature metamorphism, a condition found in subduction environments and rarely any other place. One boulder can be found just north of the Junction Office in a gully on the east side of North Gate Road. On the Summit Road toward the summit just past the Rocky Point Picnic area, you will notice a dark blue-black boulder of blue schist about 5 feet across protruding from the bank on the left side of the road.

GROUP 3—GREAT VALLEY (*MESOZOIC*) AND YOUNGER SEDIMENTARY ROCKS (*CENOZOIC*)

The third major rock sequence on and around Mt. Diablo are the thick sections of sedimentary rock formed from material derived, not from subduction to the west, but from material eroded from ancient highlands to the east, an ancient "Sierra" if you like, and proto-Klamath ranges in the north. Beginning about 10 million years ago, river, lake, and stream sediments replaced marine deposits as the sea retreated from the Great Valley for the final time.

These rocks are exposed today wrapping around the mountain with bedding dipping steeply away from the Franciscan and ophiolite core. As you drive up South Gate Road to the summit, you are driving over rocks continually increasing in age—a 190 million-year journey backward through geologic time. In the Rock City and Castle Rock areas along the south and west side of the mountain, the original flat-lying beds are now upturned and stand almost vertical. Differential weathering of alternating resistant sandstone and soft shale layers is responsible for the ridge-valley topography seen around the mountain's west, south, and east sides.

GREAT VALLEY GROUP
(*UPPER JURASSIC THROUGH CRETACEOUS*)

The name Great Valley Group refers to the thick sedimentary deposits of Upper Jurassic through Cretaceous age that were deposited in the marine basin west of the present day Sierra. The Great Valley sequence is composed mostly of deepwater marine shale, sandstone and some conglomerates accumulating to a thickness of 60,000 feet near the western margin of the present day Sacramento Valley, then thinning toward Mt. Diablo. The oldest beds (140 to 145 myo "Knoxville" in this area) were deposited on top of a remnant of ocean-ic crust (ophiolite). Great Valley deposits on-lap the Mt. Diablo area and thinner deposits intermittently covered it during this time.

CENOZOIC TERTIARY AND QUATERNARY SEQUENCES

To summarize the Cenozoic in this area, it is perhaps easiest to think of the Central Valley of California as a low elongate basin, flooded intermittently by an encroaching shallow sea, and slowly being filled by sedimentary material from the surrounding exposed land masses, primarily the "Sierra." During the last part of the Tertiary, these new highlands became the primary source area for the material found in the upper Tertiary rocks.

The Mt. Diablo area (along with the Kirby Hills to the north) seemed to represent a persistent "high," frequently underwater, but less deep than surrounding areas and periodically exposed to erosion. Many of the formations seem to shoal out on the flanks of this area and when submerged, the strata thin over the "high." The area, however, was not a "mountain" as we see it today, but rather a land of low relief. The rising of Mt. Diablo would have to wait until the Pleistocene, still far in the future.

PALEOCENE ROCKS (58–64 MILLION YEARS AGO):

There are few **Paleocene** deposits present in our area indicating that the region was probably above sea-level and undergoing erosion following the close of the Cretaceous. The only nearby rocks of this age are restricted to the north side of the mountain outside of the park.

EOCENE ROCKS (36.5–58 MYA):

During the **Eocene**, the climate warmed, resulting in heavy "ancestral Sierra" weathering that yielded large quantities of sands that washed into and across the Central Valley providing material to the Eocene deposits of Mt. Diablo. A shallow marine basin, a sandy shoreline, a swampy backwater area—all existed in this area at different times or at the same time in different places.

On the north side of the mountain, the Eocene is present in the Black Diamond Mines Regional Park. These strata contain coal beds and glass sands and have been described as a near-shore lagoonal swamp or tidal flat esturarian environment. On Mt. Diablo, Eocene deposits form the ridges of tan-colored sandy rock formations that wrap around the south and west side of the mountain. They are well exposed at Castle Rock, Rock City, Knobcone Point, and Cave Point. Sands on the south side of the mountain are characteristic of deep offshore slope deposits, shedding sands off the southwestern flank of the "Mt. Diablo high" toward an open sea to the west. Shallow near-shore deposits contain beds rich in *Turritella* fossils (marine snails).

These massive sandstone beds weather easily forming features such as wind caves and open tunnels. Rock City, easily accessible on the South Gate Road, is a good place to view these unusual features.

OLIGOCENE ROCKS (23.7–36.5 MYA):

The only **Oligocene** in the area is the Kirker Tuff on the north side of the mountain outside the park boundary.

MIOCENE ROCKS (23.7–5.3 MYA):

On the south and west sides of the mountain, the depositional contact between the **Eocene** and the **Miocene** rocks can be recognized by the abrupt change from clean, thick-bedded, light tan sandstone in the Domengine formation (Eocene) to poorly sorted, dark gray, pebbly sandstone of the marine Miocene rocks. There is a large gap in the geologic time record between these rock units, representing erosion or non-deposition.

During middle Miocene time, the general drainage was directed from the east into an open ocean to the west, a pattern similar to the deposition of the earlier Eocene. By about 10 mya (million years ago), subduction had ended in central California and there was a major change in the pattern of deposition. A highland developed to the west and the Diablo Range south of Livermore began to rise. The Mt. Diablo area began to accumulate marine and later non-marine deposits from these sources.

Now steeply tilted upward from an original horizontal orientation, the vertical beds form the prominent "hogbacks" on Fossil Ridge and Blackhawk Ridge. Building material quarried from Fossil Ridge was used to construct the summit museum building, and numerous clam and oyster shells can be seen in the exterior walls of that building.

These fossiliferous beds are called the Briones Formation. Following Briones deposition, the direction of sediment transport shifted again, bringing sands derived from the east, rich in volcanic material washed from the Sierran highlands. These volcanic sands have been named the Neroly formation. They form the grass-covered rounded hills immediately south of the underlying ridge-forming Briones strata on the south, and can be found on the west and north sides of the mountain as well.

Andesitic Neroly sandstone alters easily, and in most places the sand grains are coated with a thin layer of bluish clay that is clearly exposed on Shell Ridge in Walnut Creek. Beds rich in fossil marine shells are well exposed on Shell Ridge and in Sycamore Canyon. By around 9 million years ago, during the late Miocene, the sea again receded from the Mt. Diablo area, marking a permanent change from marine deposition to non-marine stream and lake deposition.

One of the nine million-year-old stream deposits on the south side of the mountain has captured and preserved an abundant and diverse collection of animal fossils. The Blackhawk Ranch Quarry has yielded numerous vertebrate fossils of horses, rhinos, camels, and smaller animals. A large mastodon skull, a *Gomphotherium*, has been removed from this site. All give evidence that late Miocene mammals abounded in the newly created forests and flood plains stretching away to low hills to the west and south. There are several volcanic tuff deposits in the late Miocene and Pliocene derived from the volcanic fields of Sonoma County. There was still no Mt. Diablo at the time.

PLIO-PLEISTOCENE TO RECENT ROCKS (5.3 MYA TO PRESENT):

Non-marine deposits continued to collect in the area during **Pliocene** time (1.67–5.3 mya). It was during **Plio-Pleistocene** time, by 4 mya and continuing to the present, that Mt. Diablo was formed as a topographic feature. From that time on, Mt. Diablo has been feeding erosional materials into surrounding valleys. Pliocene sources were predominantly Great Valley rocks. Pleistocene sources were predominantly Franciscan, indicating unroofing and erosion of deeper Franciscan terranes. The 4.83 million-year-old Lawlor Tuff is a widespread marker bed around the mountain. The fact that it was laid down on a relatively flat landscape and is now steeply folded indicates that Mt. Diablo must have begun its growth after the tuff was deposited.

FORMING THE MOUNTAIN— MT. DIABLO'S TECTONIC HISTORY

Although Mt. Diablo is old in terms of its rock history, it is very young as a topographic feature. The rising of Mt. Diablo to its present height is the result of a complex interplay of tectonic forces operating during the last few million years. Mt. Diablo started growing in Pliocene time, but did not start its major growth until late Pleistocene time, about 500,000 years ago. These geologic processes have created a complex uplifted compressional fold. The mountain is continually undergoing the sculpturing effects of erosion and is still rising today at the rate of 1 to 3 millimeters a year.

Recently, two ideas have been suggested to account for the uplift and folding of Mt. Diablo. Both involve the recognition that the Mt. Diablo region has been undergoing compressional stress over the past few million years. However, this compression and resultant folding may be caused by two different stress mechanisms.

The first scenario proposes that the development of the Mt. Diablo tectonic block was the result of compressional forces acting in a SW–NE direction forming a compressional fold with an anticlinal NW–SE axis. A northeast dipping thrust fault broke the fold and plunged under the mountain. This thrust fault is also pulling the San Ramon Valley and

Livermore Valley blocks under the mountain. The under-thrusting block, moving in a northeast direction, is lifting and folding the mountain above it. The Mt. Diablo block itself is referred to as a back-thrust block riding up the underlying thrust plane and being folded in the process.

These compressional forces are owed to the fact that during the past two million years or so, there has been a small compressional component to the large scale San Andreas strike-slip fault system. The Calaveras, Concord, and Greenville faults are recognized as the easternmost strands of the San Andreas fault system. Conventional theory suggests that the north-south slip on the Calaveras Fault dies out near Danville and jumps eastward to the Concord Fault. The earthquake swarm near Danville in 1990 is cited as an indication of a series of ruptures in the transition zone between the two faults. (See figure 3.)

The second scenario requires compression as well, but the compressional forces acting on Mt. Diablo are generated by horizontal movement along roughly north-south trending faults (in this case the Greenville–Morgan Territory Fault on the east side of the mountain and the Concord fault on the northwest side). Rock caught between two parallel moving faults will undergo compression.

In this case, the folding of Mt. Diablo is the result of the contraction that is driven by a transfer of slip from the Greenville Fault to the Concord fault. Most of the slip transfer occurs across the Mt. Diablo anticline. When the northward development of the Greenville–Morgan Territory Fault is blocked by impinging on the stable Central Valley block, relief of the stress must jump west to the Concord Fault. Across Mt. Diablo, the stress is relieved by the development of a blind thrust fault under the mountain. The westward propagation of the tip of the blind thrust uplifts and folds the strata above. The trace of the

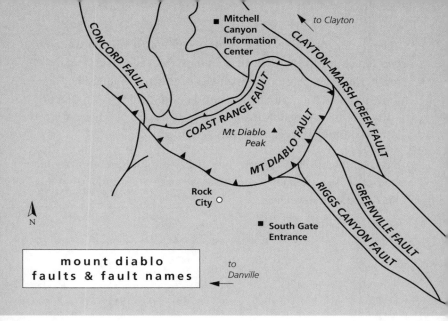

Figure 3.

fault plane remains underground and does not reach the surface. It is estimated the fault plane may be as deep as 10 miles beneath the mountain.

The realization that blind thrust faults have been responsible for some of the strongest earthquakes in California (including the Coalinga quake in 1983, and the Northridge quake in 1994 that killed 61 people, injured thousands, and caused $20 billion in damage) has spurred the USGS to study the populous East Bay more carefully. The recognition of the possible existence of a blind thrust fault under Mt. Diablo has resulted in the issuance of an advisory by the USGS in September of 1999 predicting a four-percent probability of a 6.7 or larger earthquake occurring on the blind thrust fault underlying the mountain.

There is one prominent southeast-directed thrust fault on the mountain separating the Franciscan from the Great Valley sedimentary rocks. This fault, commonly mapped as the Mt. Diablo Thrust Fault or the Mt. Diablo Fault (not to be confused with the blind Mt. Diablo Thrust Fault), is probably inactive and some geologists believe it was formed during Cretaceous to early Tertiary time.

It is clear that geology is not a static field—our interpretation of the landscape is continually changing as we learn more and look at the landscape with new ideas.

road log along north gate road, south gate road, and summit road

Log 1—South Gate Road to Junction Office

Log 2—North Gate Road to Junction Office

Log 3—Summit Road from Junction Office to Summit

LOG 1—SOUTH GATE ROAD: Danville Entrance

0.00   Set odometer to "zero" at entrance to South Gate Road as you turn north off Mt. Diablo Scenic Blvd. For the first half mile you will be crossing non-marine strata of **Pliocene** and **upper-Miocene** age. The beds are almost vertical and you will be traveling 90 degrees to the strike of the beds, progressing over increasingly older strata as you

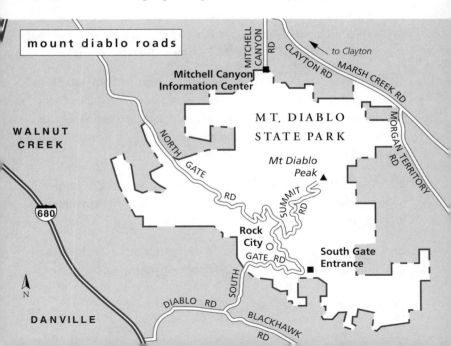

proceed north past the Athenian School.

These beds are the same age as those containing the Blackhawk Ranch Quarry mammal fossils. Up ahead you can see the light tan stratified rocks of the **Eocene** "Domengine" at the top of the ridge.

0.6 The rounded hills to the right with scattered oaks and newly built homes are mapped as part of the **Diablo Formation**. The Diablo Formation represents the transition from non-marine to marine in this area. You will continue in the Diablo Formation for about four-tenths of a mile, past the first sharp turn to the left until you reach the **second** sharp turn to the left.

0.95 Here you take the second sharp turn to the left. Almost all of the maps show this as the upper boundary of the **Neroly Formation**. The Neroly sandstone and shale is brownish in color along the road-cuts and contains rich fossil clam beds, well exposed farther east in Sycamore Canyon. The material making up the rock is volcanic debris in origin, material eroded from the Sierran highlands.

1.15 Boundary Gate to park. You will traverse eastward (and occasionally northward) and begin your climb up the south flank of Mt. Diablo. You will continue to travel over increasingly older Neroly for the next one-third mile, expressed as rounded grass-covered hills with oak trees prominent.

2.2 Final turn north in the Neroly brings into view the steep—almost vertical—chaparral-covered slope of the **Briones Formation** just ahead.

2.45 As you make a sharp turn to the right, you will begin the serious climb up the south side of Mt. Diablo, driving along the strike of the **Miocene Briones Formation**. The shallow marine sandstone beds are not only almost vertical here, they are in fact slightly overturned, which means the "underside of the beds" (facing south) is younger than the "topsides" (facing north). The beds frequently contain marine fossil shells.

As you climb up the Briones "wall," the difference in the character of the topography and plant communities between the Neroly and Briones formations is very apparent. The Neroly is represented by the adjacent grass- and oak-covered rounded hills to the south, which stand in sharp contrast to the steep chaparral-covered slope of the Briones to the north.

3.65 This is a rather spectacular overlook across Sycamore Canyon to the **"hogback ridges"** plunging down the western edge of **Blackhawk Ridge** into the canyon. Immediately to the left beside the road are corresponding beds forming **Fossil Ridge**. There are several beds with fossils exposed here, but the park does not allow "pull-outs" except in an emergency. I suggest you proceed to the **South Gate Entrance Station** just ahead and get permission to park there briefly and walk back down to the overlook.

These "hogbacks" represent the basal (oldest) beds of the Briones Formation. As you walk (drive) back to the entrance station you will be in an underlying siltstone unit, with pebbly siltstones and conglomerates. Less resistant to erosion, this interval of Miocene beds forms a characteristic grassy "saddle" between the overlying Briones, and the underlying **Mid-Eocene "Domengine."**

3.80 **South Entrance Station.** After passing the entrance station, you will be entering the **mid-Eocene "Domengine Formation."** The rocks exhibit a wide variety of erosion features. As we now travel northwest away from the entrance station, the deep valley to the north (right) is formed by the West Fork of Sycamore Creek. The rocky slope across the valley is Domengine as well.

It is interesting to note that after passing the chaparral-covered Briones, we now find that the gray ("digger") pine has become a prominent tree. They seem to thrive in the sandy soils of the Domengine and their presence has been used to help map the Domengine outcrops on the north side of the mountain in Black Diamond Mines Regional Park.

4.4   This massive monolith has been called **"Gibraltar Rock."** These rocks are popular with climbers.

4.65   **Rock City**. Many short trails for exploring the interesting wind cave formations in the Domengine.

4.85   After passing the ranger's house on the right, you will be driving over rocks that are less sandy and more shaley then the massive sandstone of Rock City. During the next half mile, you will notice the trees give way to more open grassland.

5.45   **Curry Point.** There is a pull-out here at Curry Point that provides a view of the distant Sierra on a clear day and the summit of Mt. Diablo to the north. The mountain is capped by rocks of the Franciscan Assemblage that have been thrust southeastward over the **Cretaceous Great Valley shale** exposed in the east-west aligned valley immediately north of Curry Point. The large boulder lying just above the valley floor on the lower slope of the mountain probably slid down from the in-place **Franciscan** higher up the mountain. Looking north, the valley contains outcrops of Great Valley shale of upper

Cretaceous age. The Cretaceous beds are bounded on the north by the **Mt. Diablo Thrust Fault**. The fault trace on the surface is mostly covered by **landslide deposits.** Above the thrust fault is **Franciscan melange** material and farther up the hard resistant greenstone and chert forming the rocky crest of Mt. Diablo's main peak and North Peak. The protruding rock to the east of Mt. Diablo summit is Devil's Pulpit, a resistant chert outcrop.

After leaving Curry Point, you will be driving west, parallel and just above the contact between Upper Cretaceous Great Valley rocks (in this case a brown-colored shale) to the north and the younger Eocene "Meganos" (lighter-colored sandy shale) on which you are driving.

6.2   Here you turn to cross the open valley to the north. You will be crossing over the **Cretaceous/Eocene contact** here. This contact is a major unconformity with a hiatus of about 10 million years where the entire record of Paleocene history is missing. That unconformity marks the boundary between the **age of mammals (Cenozoic)** and the **age of the dinosaurs (Mesozoic)**.

6.4   **Mount Diablo Thrust Fault.** After passing a sign that says "2000 Feet," you will notice on your right a slight dip in the surface of the road bank with a sign that says "Authorized Vehicles Only" and "Helioport" (this is the second "Helioport" sign). If you examine the road bank (looking east), left of the "Authorized Vehicles Only" sign, you will find blocks of Franciscan chert and greenstone. To the right of the "Helioport" sign, down the road about 20 to 30 feet, these rock types are missing; instead you will see an exposure of brown shale in the road cut. These two rock types, Franciscan to the north and Upper Cretaceous Great Valley to the south, are separated by the Mt. Diablo Thrust Fault. Franciscan rocks have been thrust up to the southeast and over the younger Cretaceous Great Valley strata.

From this point to the Junction Office, you will be driving in Franciscan melange, where large blocks of typical Franciscan rocks are exposed along the side of the road. The red-brown soils are characteristic of the iron-rich greenstone that makes up much of the Franciscan on the mountain. Red radiolarian cherts, along with lesser amounts of shale and graywacke are also exposed.

7.0   Junction Office—End

LOG 2—NORTH GATE ROAD: Walnut Creek Entrance

0.00   Set odometer to "zero" at the **North Gate entrance kiosk**. For the next 1.6 miles you will be traveling over **Upper Cretaceous Great Valley** sedimentary rocks made up mostly of shale with some sandstone beds. The topography consists of low rounded hills cut by the Little Pine Creek running parallel to the road. Beds dip steeply to the southwest.

1.6   Enter park at this point. Continue traveling on Upper Cretaceous rocks. The top of the hills to the right (west) is **Eocene** in age.

2.0   As you turn left and then right, crossing a stream gully, you will notice gray-green rocks along the left side of the road cut just before you cross over the gully. The gray-green rock outcrop itself is a badly weathered exposure of **serpentine**, forming the westernmost edge of the long **serpentine** band that runs prominently east-west across the mountain. The fault that separates the serpentine from the Franciscan is probably expressed topographically by the east-trending gully at this point. The fault plane dips down and to the north. The serpentine is separated from the upper Cretaceous Great Valley beds (on which you have been traveling) by a major fault, the **Mt. Diablo Thrust Fault.**

As you cross the gully and round the next bend (again driving briefly on the Upper Cretaceous shale), you will notice a large rock outcrop ahead on the left side of the road. It is at this point you once again cross the **Mt. Diablo Thrust Fault** (Cretaceous Great Valley to the west, Franciscan to the east) and will continue in the Franciscan from this point on. The large imposing rock outcrop is a greenstone outcrop (not serpentine).

As you continue to drive south, keep an eye out for the typical assemblage of rocks you find in the Franciscan Complex—**greenstone** (basalt), **red radiolarian chert, graywacke,** and **shale** along with a few blocks of dark blue **schist.** In this area, these varied rock types are enclosed in a **melange.** The **Mt. Diablo Thrust Fault** continues to run parallel to and west of the road, separating Franciscan rocks on the east from Cretaceous Great Valley rocks on the west.

3.2   Camel Rock. As you approach 3.2 miles, watch for Camel Rock—a rock outcrop that (with the help of a little imagination) resembles the outline of a single hump camel. You will first see it ahead and up a short slope.

3.35   Just past Camel Rock, you go over a rise of a hill and you will notice ranch buildings ahead. The prominent ridge across the valley to the west is made up of lower-Eocene-age sandstone and shale while the valley below on the west side of the **Mt. Diablo Thrust Fault** is Upper Cretaceous and part of the **Great Valley Group.** The Mt. Diablo Thrust Fault itself runs along the slope about halfway between the road and the creek bed. The hills are relatively treeless, typical of an unstable soil such as a melange.

4.4   As you round a bend at this point you will notice a pile of rocks ahead. This rock formation is called **Turtle Rock**. It is made of radiolarian chert and from this perspective doesn't look much like a turtle. Better views later.

4.8   **Turtle Rock** (behind the gate to "Diablo Ranch" on the right). We are now traveling on material formed by a large **landslide**. This material also encloses blocks of Franciscan rock types and looks a lot like **melange** topography; it is often difficult to distinguish the two landforms from each other.

You will be traveling on **landslide** material containing large blocks of **Franciscan** rocks up several major switchbacks for about 1½ miles. Look back as you go and you will see that Turtle Rock is aptly named (shell to the south and head to the north).

6.4   By the time you reach the ranger's house, you will be out of the landslide and back into **Franciscan melange topography**.

6.65   Notice the small blue-black boulder in the gully on the left side of the road about 100 yards before you reach the Junction Ranger Station. This is **"blue schist."** This sodic amphibole schist is common in the Franciscan melange and is named for the noticeable blue color of the mineral **glaucophane**. Blue schists are largely altered basalt and reflect a history of **hi-pressure/low- temperature metamorphism,** and on Mt. Diablo are about 165 million years old (younger than the greenstone, but older than the graywacke).

6.7   **Junction Office—End**

LOG 3—SUMMIT ROAD: Junction Ranger Station to Summit

0.00 **Set your odometer to "zero"** when you turn up Summit Road at the Junction Ranger Station. The entire drive to the summit will be in the Franciscan Assemblage. Watch for the characteristic exposures of Franciscan type rocks including **red cherts, greenstone (basalt),** and a few outcrops of **graywacke** and **blueschist.** The soils are typically red-brown in color due to the high iron content of the parent rocks. Between here and near Toyon Picnic area the drive will be through Franciscan **melange**.

0.55 As you round the curve (turning right) after passing the **Rocky Point Picnic area**, you will notice a dark blue-black boulder about 5 feet across protruding from the bank on the left side of the road ahead. This is one of the rather common **blueschist blocks** (one of the so-called "Exotic Blocks") found in the Franciscan. Blueschist is largely altered basalt and reflect a history of hi-pressure/low-temperature metamorphism and on Mt. Diablo are about 165 million years old (younger than the greenstone, but older than the graywacke). The adjacent tan-colored rocks are sandstone and siltstone.

1.2 To the left you will pass a prominent exposure of red **radiolarian chert.** If you pull off at the turnout, you will also be able to look out over the ridges of younger rocks to the south. As you look south and southwest, the valley below contains Cretaceous rocks bordered on the north by the Mt. Diablo Thrust Fault and on the south by younger Eocene age rocks that include the yellow-tan sandstone exposed around Rock City and Castle Rocks. The more distant row of ridges (Fossil Ridge, Blackhawk Ridge, and Oyster Point) are Miocene in age and are quite fossiliferous.

If you look to the north, you will see the rugged "chert/greenstone" capped summit of Mt. Diablo.

1.5   At about 1.5 miles, you will leave the melange part of the Franciscan and the chert and greenstone outcrops become more frequent.

2.0   Around 2.0 miles, on the right side of the road and continuing for another 0.2 miles, is a major (and typical) outcrop of sheared and broken **greenstone** (basalt).

2.35   Pull out on left at **Juniper Camp Ground**. Good views to the west. You will be looking out over the San Ramon Valley and the towns of Danville, Alamo and Walnut Creek (left to right). The Calaveras Fault runs down the valley. The ridge on the far side of the valley is Las Trampas Ridge and is made up of Miocene age rocks similar to the Miocene age rocks on Mt. Diablo including highly fossiliferous sandstone beds.

3.3   Another good exposure of **greenstone**, highly sheared, with slickensides visible.

3.6   As you make a sharp turn to the left, you will see more chert and greenstone rocks toward the north. These rocks are resistant to erosion and are responsible for the rugged topography. The red rock on the right as you pull out of your turn is thin-bedded radiolarian chert with interbeds of reddish shale. Continue to the summit.

4.5   Summit parking lot. The summit museum has excellent geology displays. A short walk along the Summit Fire Interpretive Trail is also recommended. A quarter-mile walk along the northside to the overlook platform will provide an opportunity to inspect greenstone, graywacke, red chert, and a small amount of shale up close. The quarry you see to the north is producing diabase (part of the Mt. Diablo Ophiolite) for crushed rock used in the construction of roadbeds.

commonly asked questions on the geology of mount diablo

Is Mt. Diablo a volcano?

No. Although basaltic lava rock can be found on the mountain, the lava was formed far at sea, upwelling from deep in the earth through fissures in the ocean crust.

How high is the mountain?

3,849 feet. The summit is actually inside the museum.

What kind of rock makes up the summit?

The hard resistant rock on the summit is mostly *greenstone* (a slightly altered form of basalt, a common igneous rock that makes up much of the upper part of the ocean crust) and hard reddish *chert* with minor amounts of graywacke sandstone and shale. The exposed rock that you can stand on inside the summit museum is greenstone.

Why does it stand up higher than the surrounding area?

The rocks have been folded and lifted by compressional stresses in the earth's crust. The greenstone and chert on the two main peaks are very resistant to erosion compared to many of the rocks in the surrounding areas and thus stand higher.

Is Mt. Diablo still rising?

The stresses that folded and raised the mountain are still at work and the mountain continues to slowly rise—about .1 inch a year—while the forces of weathering and erosion try to keep pace.

How old is the mountain?

The oldest rocks on the mountain are the greenstones in the mountain's core formed about 190 million years old. But the mountain, as a topographic feature, has been seriously rising only for the past 500,000 years.

Is there any gold or silver here?

Minor amounts of gold and silver associated with small copper deposits on the north side of the mountain were prospected, but production was not economical.

Are the mercury mines still in operation?

No. Mining operations stopped in the early 1970s after approximately $1,500,000 worth of mercury had been extracted.

What are they quarrying on the north side?

Diabase. Diabase is a dark igneous rock of fine crystalline texture. It is used primarily for building stones and crushed rock for roadbeds.

Are there dinosaur bones in any of the rocks? Did they live here?

No to both. The Mt. Diablo region was under the ocean during the Jurassic and Cretaceous. The closest dinosaur bones to us were found near Pacheco Pass in central California.

What about the bones at the Blackhawk Museum?

The quarry at Blackhawk is one of the richest mammal bone beds in the United States, second only to La Brea in Los Angeles. Bones from 7 million-year-old horses, camels, rhinos, and mastodons have been found here—but these are much younger than dinosaurs, which died out over 60 million years ago. The bones (only fragments are found, no complete skeletons) were preserved in stream deposits.

How old are the fossils in the building blocks of the Summit Building?

The clams, oysters, and other fossil shells in the building stones of the summit building came from the "Briones Formation" of Miocene age near Fossil Ridge and are about 12 million years old.

How are the caves formed at Rock City?

Although often called Wind Caves, they are only indirectly due to the wind. During the rainy season, rainwater with dissolved carbon dioxide from the air seeps into the rocks. The water is a very weak acid and slowly dissolves the calcium carbonate cement that had been holding the sand grains together. The hot dry days of summer would draw the water to the surface of the rock where it evaporated and left behind the cement it had dissolved from deeper in the rock. After centuries of wet winters and dry summers, the inside of the rock had only a little cement, while the outside had a hard crust of sand grains tightly cemented. As wind and rain continued to beat on the faces of the rocks, holes developed in the crust. This exposed the loosely cemented grains underneath, which erode much faster than the surface, so that holes enlarged into little caves behind the hard crust. Very little of the hard crust remains on the surface of these rocks today.

hiking on mount diablo

introduction

UNDERSTANDING THE TRAIL SIGNS

The identification of the hiking trails on Mount Diablo has been much improved of late owing to the signage project spearheaded by the Mount Diablo Interpretive Association. Nearly 400 signs have been added as part of the effort begun in 1993 by MDIA.

The signs on Mount Diablo follow the uniform format prescribed for use in all California State parks. The format has confused more than one visitor who has hastily read only the larger words on the sign. The name of the trail you are on is the trail name, specified in relatively small horizontal type near the top of the sign. The name that appears vertically in larger type (usually another trail but sometimes a park boundary) shows where the trail you are on leads to if you follow it in the direction of the arrow above the sign; the word 'TO', in small letters, is important. The mileage to the destination is specified at the bottom.

Here is a simplified sample to the left.

The sign shows that you are on Angel Kerley Road, and that if you go .43 miles to the left you will arrive at the junction with Diablo Ranch Road.

WEATHER

Weather changes frequently on the mountain, so it is recommended that you dress in layers. The mountain gets around 20 inches of rain a year, almost all of it between the months of October and April. The higher elevations usually get at least a dusting of snow 2 or 3 times a year from the coldest of these winter storms.

A WORD ABOUT LYME DISEASE

Lyme disease in California is caused by the bite of the Western Black-legged Tick, found throughout rural California, including Mount Diablo. The first sign of Lyme disease is usually (but not always) a rash that occurs about a week after contact, followed by flu-like symptoms, then by pain and/or swelling in major joints. Ticks climb to the edge of vegetation, waiting for an animal or human host to brush against them so that they can attach themselves. To prevent being bitten, wear long pants, long-sleeved clothing, and shoes covering the toes. Use insect repellent on shoes, socks, pants, and shirt. Since it may take a day or more to transmit the bacteria for Lyme disease, prompt removal of ticks should prevent contraction of the illness. Grasp the tick with a tissue or tweezers, and gently pull it from the skin; do not try to twist or 'unscrew' it. If symptoms of Lyme disease do appear, see a doctor. Most cases of Lyme disease can be successfully treated by a course of antibiotics, but early treatment is important.

short, pleasant hikes (1/2 hour to 2 hours)

Here are some easy but rewarding walks on the mountain. All of the walks are relatively level with some minor to moderate climbing. The footing is firm, and the trails can be negotiated in comfortable walking shoes. To find the trailheads, consult the accompanying map.

1 FIRE INTERPRETIVE TRAIL (SUMMIT)

Trailhead: On north side of road by picnic table, just at end of one-way road on its descent from summit, above "lower summit" parking lot.

Trail statistics: Loop of 0.7 miles, level (follows contour; gentle climb at end). Completely encircles summit of mountain. Easy walk, one half hour without stops. Drinking water and toilets at lower summit parking lot.

Description: A must for both the casual visitor and the nature student. The incomparable views of the California landscape far below are enhanced by the framing foreground of the unusual trailside vegetation, with fine flower displays in spring and early summer. Of primary interest are the various stages of vegetative recovery following the great fire of 1977. Spectacular rock outcrops of ancient Franciscan Complex rocks abound. The trail was built by the Youth Conservation Corps; the first one-third is paved and is wheelchair accessible up to the Ransome Point overlook, a good place to spot distant landmarks from comfortable benches.

2 FOSSIL RIDGE

Trailhead: Uplands Picnic Area, adjacent to South Gate Road, at junction with small side road to Live Oak Campground. Trail starts as small road, badly paved, climbing hill steeply; there is a simple gate, sign barring public vehicles.

Trail Statistics: 1.2-mile round trip. Short, steep climb at beginning. Easy walk thereafter.

Description: The initial climb opens up imposing vistas of the massive main peak of the mountain, as well as of San Ramon Valley in the opposite direction. The road parallels the crest of Fossil Ridge—the adventurous may wish to scramble up to the rocky ridge, a sharp hogback (tilted sandstone layer with adjacent layers eroded away) with interesting exposed fossils, rock-garden-like appearance. Dramatic view of Black Hawk Ridge strata across Sycamore Canyon from small path beyond end of road. Good bird watching.

3 MITCHELL CANYON

Trailhead: End of Mitchell Canyon Road, north entrance to park, near the town of Clayton. Park in staging area (water and toilets).

Trail Statistics: Level for the first two miles except for a slight gain in elevation at the beginning.

Description: The following description is keyed to ten numbered posts along the first mile of the trail.

1. Mitchell Canyon Trail begins within an oak woodland. Blue oak, the dominant species, is deciduous, dropping its leaves in the fall. Wild oats, introduced to California by Spanish missionaries, fill the grassy areas. The gray-green needle-leaved trees upslope are Coulter Pine, producers of the heaviest cones of all the pines. Standing above the trees is Mitchell Rock, an outcrop of pillow basalt, formed during the Jurassic period when this region was part of a sea floor in the Pacific Ocean.

2. Downslope, on the right side of the road, is a large coast live oak, one of the most common trees on Mount Diablo. Over two hundred years old, this tree was selected by the Daughters of the American Revolution to commemorate the bicentennial of the U.S. Constitution and the men and women who worked for its adoption. Live oaks are evergreen, with leaves remaining year round. Their small, hard, leathery leaves conduct photosynthesis at a low rate. This prevents wilting and loss of moisture during California's dry, hot summers.

3. Mitchell Creek lies below you, winding around a former man-made pond. Non-native species of mustard, thistle, and poison hemlock fill the former pond site. On the slopes above the pond site, California sagebrush, blue bush lupine, California poppies (the state flower), and other native plants abound. Above the stream course, clumps of mistletoe, parasitic to live oaks, hang from the oak trees. Although toxic to humans, mistletoe bears sticky white berries on which many birds love to feed.

4. Bush (sticky) monkeyflower, bearing funnel-shaped yellow-orange flowers that remain through spring and summer, grows in profusion on the slope adjacent to the trail. Common on dry hillsides, monkeyflower leaves have a sticky coating that minimizes moisture loss during hot days. Native Californians once used the leaves to cover cuts and scrapes. Miner's lettuce grows nearby in moist shaded areas during the rainy season. Early settlers and Gold Rush miners ate the small leaves of miner's lettuce when fresh vegetables were unavailable, hence the name.

5. Growing near the post is coffeeberry. Variable in form, this shrub has no relationship to the beverage but produces dark purple fruits that encase coffeebean-shaped seeds. The seeds are bitter, but many

mammals eat and disperse them. Observe the accumulation of coyote scat at the base of the plant, near the post. You might find berries as well as hair in the scat. Coyotes are omnivores (consume both plants and animals) and like to deposit their scat in open, flat areas where trails cross or dip down a little knoll.

6. Willows, alders, and an occasional Fremont cottonwood line the banks of Mitchell Creek, forming a riparian (streamside) community. Tangled layers of shrubs are covered with climbing vines of California grape, wild cucumber, blackberries, and clematis. California quail, our state bird, hide in the thick underbrush. As the day warms, butterflies flit amid the foliage. Often California sisters, mourning cloaks, and swallowtail butterflies add splashes of color along this section of the trail.

7. Shady areas along the trail are host to soap plant and the Mount Diablo globe tulip (fairy lantern). In the spring, shimmering lemon-yellow globe-shaped flowers mark the location of the globe tulips. Endemic (found only here) to Mount Diablo, they are one of many wildflowers found in Mitchell Canyon. Nearby, loosely crimped leaves emerge from the bulb of the soap plant. After the spring growing period, only brushy brown hairs remain, covering the starchy bulb. Native Californians used the bulbs of soap plants as food as well as for glue, soap, and brushes.

8. The small tree with silvery white bark is a California buckeye. Buckeyes drop their leaves during August and September, thereby conserving moisture. In the spring, buckeye flowers appear as large, cream-colored upright spikes at the ends of branch tips. In the fall, baseball-sized pear-shaped fruit pods, containing glossy brown seeds, hang from the branch tips. Native Californians crushed buckeye

seeds, tossed them into slow-moving streams, thereby stupefying fish, which then floated to the surface.

9. Coyote bush lines the road here. Evergreen all year, with small, fragrant leaves, coyote bush has separate (dioecious) male and female plants. Creamy disc-shaped flowers distinguish male plants, whereas the flowers of female plants are white. As you continue along the trail vegetation becomes less dense. Western fence lizards may dart across the trail. Each male "blue-belly" establishes a territory, defending it by bluff and fighting. Their bluff posture resembles push-ups, which show the blue markings.

10. The trail begins to climb as you round this corner. Rising above you are south-facing rocky slopes covered with chaparral vegetation. Hard-leaved evergreen shrubs dominate chaparral. Adapted to nutrient poor soils and harsh conditions, leaves are stiff, thick, and often have a waxy coating. Toyon (California holly or Christmas berry) inhabit the spine of the ascending slope. Dark-green serrated (holly like) leaves, contrasted with bright orange-red berries in late fall and early winter, earned the plant its common names.

4 PINE POND

Trailhead: Not long after your car starts its climb on North Gate Road, you will note a distant ridge that comes in from the right to meet the winding road. After a particularly sharp curve, the highway rises steeply toward the ridge, access to which is provided by two bright aluminum gates on opposite sides of the road just after the white 3.0-mile marker. Limited parking is available in front of the lower (western) gate, which is the actual trailhead, or at the elevation sign beyond. No facilities.

Trail Statistics: The round trip to the pond is only 1.6 miles, with a 400-ft. drop just before Pine Pond (and, of course, a 400-ft. climb on the way back). Trails up and down Pine Canyon from Pine Pond can be explored as far as one desires. Spend an hour, or spend the day.

Description: The graded road crosses an oak savannah, with fine views of the gentle foothills of Mt. Diablo—a good place just to lie in the grass to contemplate the sky. A sharp left at the next junction drops you down to the banks of the little lake, a habitat for a myriad of flying, swimming, crawling, and jumping creatures that constitute an incomparable living museum.

5 JUNIPER TRAIL

Trailhead: At Laurel Dell Group Picnic Area, in Juniper Campground, just where the campground loop load returns to meet the Summit Road. Drinking water and toilets.

Trail Statistics: 1.2 miles to lower summit parking lot, 720-ft. elevation gain.

Description: A nicely graded, intimate trail built by the Youth Conservation Corps just before the 1977 fire. Switchbacks (avoid slippery shortcuts) facilitate the climb through the dark oak–laurel forest, survivor of many a fire, to Moses Rock Ridge. Bear right through vigorous chaparral to reach interesting rock outcrops supporting a variety of stunted, tundra-like plants. Fine views through the silvery branches of fire-scarred chaparral. Trail crosses main road and winds up at parking lot. Return trip is all downhill. Wonderful for photography. Allow two hours.

6 DEER FLAT ROAD (JUNIPER CAMP)

Trailhead: At far end of Juniper Camp loop road. There is a parking area just at the point where road begins its turn at the far end of the loop. Facilities in campground.

Trail Statistics: Deer Flat Road runs an essentially level course for 0.4 miles to its junction with Burma Road. This part is a very easy walk.

Description: The pleasant walk highlights fine views into San Ramon Valley across grassy slopes, emerald green in the springtime, with some of the most spectacular California poppy displays on the mountain. The thick grasses thrive in the deep soil of the steep slumps below you, erosion products of the summit rocks. Each season brings new color surprises—the golden grasses against the deep blue sky in summer, and the same grasses, now a silvery grey, bathed in the mists of winter.

7 CASTLE ROCK

Trailhead: By large "Castle Rock Park" sign at the end of Castle Rock Road (an extension of Oak Grove Road, Walnut Creek). Park in spaces in front of sign. Trailhead is opposite the horse stables, at "Diablo Foothills Regional Trail Access" sign. Facilities in Castle Rock Park; foot traffic through privately leased park is allowed.

Trail Statistics: A level walk of 1.5 miles (one way) takes you to the best overview of Castle Rock, spectacularly eroded pinnacle looming high above. A Regional Park trail from the trailhead skirts the Castle Rock Park facilities and meets the old stagecoach road to Mt. Diablo. Follow this road along Pine Creek; it runs along the boundary of Diablo Foothills Regional Park up to the State Park gate and to the Castle Rock overlook just beyond.

Description: Not far beyond the trailhead the road enters a cool, mature oak forest, a refuge in the hot days of summer. Pine Creek meanders through the forested meadows, and the road crosses the stream several times, requiring some careful balancing on stones in the stream. Butterflies abound in sunlit clearings. Raptor nests can sometimes be spotted with binoculars in the sandstone cavities of Castle Rock high above.

Castle Rock. *Courtesy Bob Walter/IDG Films.*

8 DONNER CREEK

Courtesy Tom Harris.

Trailhead: From direction of Concord, drive through Clayton to Regency Woods. Turn right on Regency Drive and drive to the dead end, with parking on the street beyond the last houses. Walk down to the trail below; the park gate is a short distance toward the mountain. No facilities.

Trail Statistics: 0.9 miles, one way, on level road. An easy walk, but road is muddy in winter and early spring.

Description: A popular trail with local residents—families with strollers, joggers, kids on bikes. The attractive environment is dominated by the view of the principal peaks of the park, rising sharply from the meadows at the base. In spring in particular, the sight of the rushing water, of Donner Creek meandering through flower-strewn emerald green grasslands is unforgettable. The road eventually enters an oak savannah and thereafter reaches the site of Donner (Hetherington) Cabin, an early pioneer residence.

9 SITE OF MOUNTAIN HOUSE

Trailhead: At upper end of loop road, Junction Picnic Area, opposite ranger station at junction of North Gate and South Gate Roads.

Trail Statistics: Junction Trail joins Summit Trail after 0.2 miles; the site is about 200 yards beyond on Summit Trail. A steady climb of 200 feet. Facilities at Sunset Picnic Area and the Junction Ranger Station.

Description: You are on the old stagecoach road that went up to Mountain House, a resort and weekend goal for Bay Area residents some 100 years ago. As you climb toward the site, the distant views of the coastal ranges slowly vanish, and you enter an imposing bowl-like enclosure in the heart of the mountain, encircled by grassy cliffs and the wilderness forest. Today the wide, level site is used to store park maintenance materials; no trace is left of the old hotel. You will have to let your imagination picture the excitement that the arrival of the stagecoach must have created a century ago.

10 SENTINEL ROCK

Trailhead: From South Gate Road, drive down into Live Oak Campground (Rock City area). Park in picnic area and walk up the paved loop road to campsite No. 20. The trail begins just behind it.

Trail Statistics: The distance to the top of Sentinel Rock is only a few hundred yards, but the walk is a bit of a scramble and a stiff climb of about 200 feet, most of it up the carved steps of Sentinel Rock. Facilities in campground.

Description: Sentinel Rock is one of the most popular destinations in

the park; yet, for such a prominent feature, it is extraordinarily difficult to spot. The steep (and a bit frightening) climb, aided by steel
cables, is well worth the effort, for the little fenced platform at the top
offers fine views of the weird Rock City wilderness in all directions.
The trail brings you to the very base of the rock. Here turn right on a
badly eroded trail and climb until the trail veers toward the rock on
your left. There is a maze of trails here, but the idea is to circle to the
eastern base of the rock where the stairway starts. Kids (of all ages)
will have a ball, but be sure everyone stays behind the cable barrier.
After the climb, take the opportunity to explore the astounding landscape of Rock City; there are no real trails, but you cannot get too lost.
Well-gripping shoes or boots are essential.

moderate hikes (2–4 hours)

Good hiking boots are recommended for these hikes. Carry water and
a jacket.

1 FALLS TRAIL LOOP

Trailhead: From direction of Concord, drive through Clayton to
Regency Woods. From Marsh Creek Road, turn right on Regency Drive
and drive to the dead end, with parking on the street beyond the last
houses. Walk down to the trail below; the park gate is a short distance
toward the mountain. No facilities.

Trail statistics: 5.9 miles via Donner Canyon Road and Hetherington
Loop Trail, then up Cardinet Oaks Road to Falls Trail; return loop on
section of Middle Trail. 1300-ft. climb (includes canyon crossings). In
winter and early spring, roads at lower elevation may be muddy.

moderate hikes

Falls Trail. *Courtesy Tom Harris.*

Description: In winter (rainy season) and throughout spring, the Falls Trail features several waterfalls up to 100 feet high. Spring also brings astounding displays of wildflowers, and the colorful rock formations are worth the trip at any time. (Kindly refrain from scrambling down to the falls; it is dangerous and damages the landscape.)

2 MT. OLYMPIA VIA NORTH PEAK

Trailhead: At roadside parking area, Devil's Elbow, on Summit Road just below the summit. Facilities at summit.

Trail Statistics: 4.6 miles round trip on North Peak Trail. Round trip involves total climb of 1670 feet, mostly on way back. Descent (and climb back) from North Peak to Mt. Olympia is very steep, on slippery scree.

Description: This is a trip for those who enjoy an unlimited sky above and views into distant depths below. The one-track path to Prospector's Gap is a show place for wildflowers in the spring. Mt. Olympia, itself, is like a little throne, high above the encircling landscape, where you can sit and observe the puny world below you, and beyond, the great plains of the Central Valley. In wintertime, the mists rolling up from the depths of Donner Canyon put on a great show of landscape hide-and-seek.

3 TWIN PEAKS–MITCHELL ROCK LOOP

Trailhead: Same as Hike No. 1. Beyond park gate, head right toward Back Canyon.

Trail Statistics: A 4.9-mile loop incorporating Eagle Peak, Mitchell Rock, and Coulter Pine Trails. Start of Eagle Peak Trail is reached by sections of Bruce Lee and Back Creek Roads; its beginning may be a little faint, a few feet from the spot where the Coulter Pine Trail takes off, heading uphill opposite a downed oak tree. At first the trail parallels Back Creek Road. Climb of 1220 feet.

Description: This is a wonderfully scenic loop at any time of year, passing through several distinct habitat zones: meadow lands, oak savannah, rocky summits, and a fine stand of Coulter Pines. The Eagle Peak Trail climbs steadily to meet the Mitchell Rock Trail at the crescent of Twin Peaks. Visitors have forged a maze of informal trails, but stick to the crest to descend to the lower Twin Peak, and you won't have any trouble. Pause to admire the brilliantly colored rocks at the summit and the venerable great-berried manzanitas, survivors of many fires, with exquisite blooms in January and February. Take care—Twin Peaks has dangerous vertical drop-offs. When Mitchell Rock Trail changes into a fire road entering the bottom meadows, veer right for the Coulter Pine Trail.

4 BLACK POINT LOOP

Trailhead: End of paved part of Mitchell Canyon Road, north entrance to park, near the town of Clayton. Park in staging area (water and toilets).

Trail Statistics: The Black Point Trail proper starts about one half mile along the Mitchell Canyon Road trail, on the right just beyond the creek crossing. It ends on Red Road, and the loop is completed by taking Mitchell Canyon Road back to the trailhead—or, better yet, by taking the small trail which parallels the road. The loop is 4.8 miles long, and the climb is 1190 feet.

Description: An outstanding journey through a hidden, little-known corner of the park, spanning several life zones, culminating at the chaparral-covered summit of Black Point. From here a truly unique perspective of central Contra Costa County is obtained. Watch for trailside "glory holes" during descent from Black Point. In spring the return trail paralleling Mitchell Canyon Road often shelters fine displays of the endemic Mt. Diablo globe lily. Wear light-colored protective clothing to combat ticks.

5 BALANCING ROCK AND KNOBCONE POINT

Trailhead: Paved parking pull-out at Curry Point, South Gate Road. No facilities.

Trail Statistics: 4.5 miles round trip, level except for a few ups and downs. Easy walk.

Description: Knobcone Point Road follows the crest of the tilted strata of Domengine sandstone, culminating with the teetering wall known as Balancing Rock. This feature has been faithfully reproduced on a full scale and forms the display focus at Walnut Creek's Lindsay Wildlife Museum. Beyond Balancing Rock, and just before the park boundary gate, follow the spur road to the right; this takes you to a most interesting display of the beneficial effect of fire (this one in 1981) upon regeneration of knobcone pines. A controlled burn of underbrush was done in 1995. At the end of the spur, to the right of the transmission line pylons, stop to admire the incredibly complex eroded sandstone landscape and the resident turkey vultures perched there or soaring overhead. Do not attempt to scale the dangerous cliffs, tempting as that may be—respect the privacy of the ticks and rattlesnakes.

6 CHASE POND AND HIDDEN POND

Trailhead: Same as Hike No. 5

Trail Statistics: 5.8 miles, mostly on dirt roads, but about 0.8 miles cross-country. Total climb of 1170 feet.

Description: The trails up to the twin Chase Ponds are well marked at intersections. The first section down Curry Canyon Road passes through a beautiful, shaded strip of riparian vegetation. A turn onto Frog Pond Road opens up rolling grasslands with some of the finest displays of massed wildflowers in the spring. Just beyond Chase Pond the road turns uphill and becomes quite faint; follow it until it meets Mountain Springs Creek, where an old cow crossing facilitates the climb up the opposite bank. Now turn back and walk cross-country in the general direction of Hidden Pond. Easily spotted among the grassy knolls, Hidden Pond is one of the mountain's beauty spots— a peaceful, lonesome pond, the quiet waters reflecting overhanging branches, the great mountain looming up behind. A short cross-country jaunt brings you to Frog Pond Road for the trip back.

7 DAN COOK CANYON

Trailhead: Park boundary on Mt. Diablo Scenic Boulevard, a little beyond the Athenian School in the hamlet of Diablo. Beyond the park gate, the road is called South Gate Road. Just beyond the gate, there is space for about four cars at the right-hand side of the road; the trail begins on the other side. Water only at Live Oak Campground.

Trail Statistics: 3.2 miles round trip to Live Oak Campground on first part of the Summit Trail. 730-ft. climb.

Description: A trail for tree lovers and rock lovers, and a great favorite of mountain bikers. The environment varies from a dry oak savannah to a shady canyon of maples, sycamores, alders, and bay trees. Farther up Dan Cook Canyon, some fascinating vistas of grotesquely eroded sandstone pinnacles open up. It will be hard for you to resist exploring the maze of Rock City beyond the Live Oak Campground with its huge coast live oaks. Here Sentinel Rock is only a few hundred feet away (see Short Hikes #10).

8 EAGLE PEAK

Trailhead: At far end of Juniper Campground loop road. There is a parking area just at the point where road begins to turn at the far end of the loop. Facilities in campground.

Trail Statistics: 6.3 miles round trip via Deer Flat Road, Meridian Ridge Road, and Eagle Peak Trail. Total climb of 1490 feet.

Description: This hike has everything, starting with the flower-strewn meadows going down to Deer Flat. Deer Flat, itself, with its symphony of bird song, is one of the mountain's memorable beauty spots. Eagle Peak Trail is an exciting hogback, often only a few feet wide, with sharp dropoffs on either side. Eagle Peak is a rocky belvedere from which to admire the expanse of Contra Costa's "Central Valley" in front of you—a good place to pause for lunch.

9 SYCAMORE CANYON LOOP

Trailhead: Same as Hike No. 5.

Trail Statistics: 3.4-mile loop using Knobcone Point, Black Hawk, and Sycamore Creek Roads, then connector trail back to Knobcone Point Trail. 580-ft. climb on return loop.

Description: A hike to savor the colors of fall or the fog-softened mysteries of winter. The passing scene is endlessly surprising and refreshing. Initially you walk through rolling meadows with magnificent views of the Mt. Diablo massif above Curry Canyon, seen through the branches of stately oaks, which in foggy weather assume a wonderful ghost-like appearance. On clear winter days, the snowy crest of the Sierra Nevada may be admired, far beyond the great expanse of the Central Valley. The colorful leafy carpets under towering sycamore trees, deep down in Sycamore Canyon, are unforgettable. Once you find the return connector trail, about one-quarter mile beyond the junction of Black Hawk and Sycamore Creek Roads, bear to your right at two small canyon junctions, but stop to explore the peculiar sulfurous streams at the junctions.

10 OLOFSON RIDGE

Trailhead: Mitchell Canyon. Same as Hike No. 4.

Trail Statistics: 5.3-mile round trip, 1010-ft. climb.

Description: After just one mile along beautiful Mitchell Canyon, turn right on Red Road which, incongruously, climbs White Canyon. In springtime, this is the site of rarer wildflower species such as the Mt. Diablo Globe Lily and Wind Poppies. Take a sharp left onto Olofson Ridge Trail, and shortly before that starts turning toward the park boundary, follow a faint trail on your left toward the summit. Find yourself a perch on the cherty outcrops, whitewashed by the presence of fellow raptors, and immerse yourself in the world of hawks, kestrels, and turkey vultures. With the awesome chasm of Mitchell Canyon and the massive walls of Eagle Peak as background, admire the aerial acrobatics of these magnificent fliers—with luck, you may even spot a golden eagle.

Golden Eagle nest on mountain. *Courtesy Michael Sewell/Visual Pursuit.*

difficult hikes (4–8 hours)

Here are ten hikes for the experienced hiker and outdoors person. Most of the suggested hikes are loop trips which are facilitated by the longer distances. The outlined hikes are day walks, from four to eight hours long. Hiking boots are essential, and you should carry water with you. It is also suggested that you bring along the Trail Map of Mt. Diablo State Park, available for purchase at the entrance stations, Junction ranger station, Summit Visitor Center, and Mitchell Canyon Interpretive Center. Many of the trails are narrow and may not have been recently brushed, and you may run across poison oak; if you think you are susceptible, it is best to protect your limbs with appropriate clothing. Such protection is also helpful against ticks.

1 SUMMIT FROM MITCHELL CANYON (LOOP)

Trailhead: End of paved part of Mitchell Canyon Road, north entrance to park, near the town of Clayton. Park in staging area (water and toilets)—parking fee.

Trail Statistics: Take Mitchell Canyon Road to Deer Flat, Deer Flat Road to Juniper Campground, and Juniper Trail to the Lower Summit Parking Lot. The summit itself is inside the Visitor Center rotunda, a short distance uphill. Return from the Lower Parking Lot along the Summit Trail to Devil's Elbow, then to Prospectors Gap via North Peak Trail, to Murchio Gap via Bald Ridge Trail, down Back Creek Trail to the Coulter Pine Trail at the base of the mountain, and back to the trailhead. The loop is 14.0 miles long, and the total climb is 3400 feet.

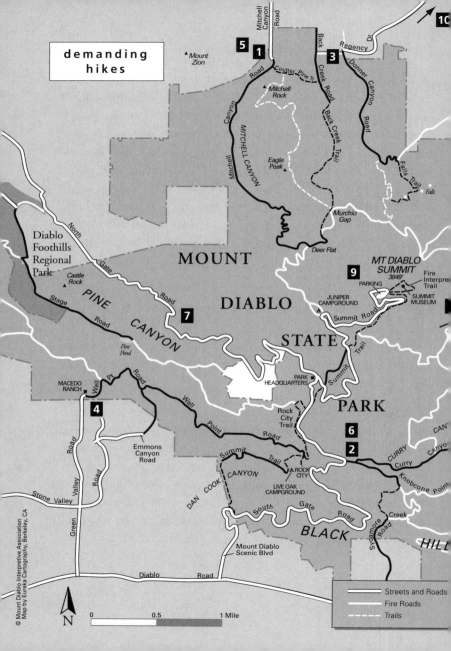

Description: This is the definitive Mt. Diablo hike—the total mountain experience. It encompasses all the park's life zones, from meadowlands to rocky summit, and the ever-changing views are simply stunning. A major portion of the loop consists of intimate single-track trails, in close encounter with the wilderness—including some poison oak which invites a cautious eye. Make no mistake: this is a challenging hike with some astonishingly steep stretches, but the result is exhilarating. In winter the meadow trails can be very mucky.

2 OYSTER POINT FROM CURRY POINT

Trailhead: Parking pull-out at Curry Point. South Gate Road. No facilities.

Trail Statistics: Follow the Knobcone Point Road to the Black Hawk Ridge Road. Turn right onto this road, descend into Sycamore Canyon, and then climb again until you reach Oyster Point Road. Follow this until it fades away, and then climb cross-country to reach the obvious Oyster Point summit (there is no trail). The round trip is 8.8 miles, and the total climb is 1750 feet on up-and-down terrain.

Description: This hike is not difficult, except for the last mad scramble up Oyster Point, around sandstone barricades and avoidable lush groves of poison oak. The summit is a Miocene sandstone hogback, where you may perch on a rocky throne of your choice to view the glorious panorama of San Ramon and the Bay Area beyond, and, in the opposite direction, the wilderness of Jackass Canyon far below. The scenery along the way to your destination is constantly changing and is a source of unending delight—meadow wildflowers in the spring, fall colors in the depths of Sycamore Canyon, and the fantastic

Domengine sandstone formations to the east of Knobcone Point at any time.

3 MT. OLYMPIA LOOP VIA MIDDLE TRAIL

Trailhead: From direction of Concord, drive through Clayton along Marsh Creek Road to Regency Woods. Turn right on Regency Drive and continue to the dead end, with parking on the street beyond the last houses. Walk down to the trail below; the park gate is a short distance toward the mountain. No facilities.

Trail Statistics: Follow Donner Canyon Road, turn left and climb steeply to Prospectors Gap; here follow the North Peak Road and Trail to Mt. Olympia. Complete the loop along Olympia Road and Trail (avoid private property), and return to the previously traversed Donner Canyon Road along the Cardinet Oaks Road, finally retracing your steps to the trailhead. The complete loop is 9.9 miles, with a climb of 3,000 feet.

Description: Mt. Olympia is one of the park's prime destinations, a rugged outcrop with fantastic views of dizzying canyons, particularly with the mists of winter. Middle Trail is a nature lover's delight, and the climb toward Prospectors Gap and descent from North Peak are— let us say—challenging.

4 WALL POINT–PINE CANYON LOOP

Trailhead: Macedo Ranch Staging Area, at the end of Green Valley Road. Green Valley Road may be reached from Stone Valley Road

(Alamo) or Diablo Road (Danville). (Both are freeway 680 exits.) Toilets, but no drinking water.

Trail Statistics: The 7.3-mile loop follows Wall Point Road to its junction with the Summit Trail, which is followed in turn up to the Barbecue Terrace Trail. This trail takes you to the Barbecue Terrace Road, which descends into Pine Canyon and eventually joins Stage Road. At an aluminum gate on the left side of Stage Road a connector trail will take you across Pine Ridge back to the Wall Point Road and the trailhead. The total climb is 1600 feet. The hike is not difficult, but roads get gummy in wet weather.

Description: Rolling meadowlands, oak savannahs, fine views of the main peak, hogbacks and sandstone fantasy, riparian habitat, and great birding—this pleasant day hike has everything. Watch for signs of recent fire activity, both prescribed and wild.

Trail. *Courtesy Liede-Marie Haitsma.*

5 LITTLE GIANT LOOP

Trailhead: End of paved part of Mitchell Canyon Road, north entrance to park near the town of Clayton. Park in staging area (water and toilets)—$2 parking fee.

Trail Statistics: This is a shorter version of Hike No. 1. A little beyond the gate at the trailhead turn left and follow the wide road eastward through the foothill meadows to Back Creek. Turn right and follow Back Creek Road and Trail to Tick Wood Trail. This path takes you to Donner Canyon Road, and a right turn soon brings you to Middle Trail, which climbs up to Prospectors Gap Road. Turn right and go to Murchio Gap, then continue on Meridian Ridge Road until you to reach Deer Flat. Take Mitchell Canyon Road back to the trailhead. This Giant Loop is 9.2 miles long with a climb of 1900 feet.

Description: The Little Giant Loop is exceptional in spring, with its mass of wildflower displays. The display is particularly striking on the Middle Trail, a fragile ecological treasure, and the Deer Flat Creek Trail, site of many rare serpentine tolerant plants. The Tick Wood Trail near the start has no more ticks than most trails. Spring rains make for soggy footing, but the mysterious oak groves with emerald grassy carpets make the struggle worthwhile.

6 PINE POND–FROG POND LOOP

Trailhead: Parking pull-out at Curry Point, South Gate Road. No facilities.

Trail Statistics: Start in a northwesterly direction on the Summit Trail, across the highway from the pull-out. Just before the trail crosses the highway, make a sharp left on an unnamed trail that descends to Wall Point Road. Go west until you reach a saddle before the climb to Wall Point itself; look out for a small connector trail on the right that descends to Barbecue Terrace Road. Then take this road (it eventually becomes Stage Road), and 0.34 miles beyond Pine Pond carefully look for a trail on the right that crosses the creek: Sunset Trail. At this trail's northern end, turn right to get eventually onto Burma Road. Follow this all the way to Deer Flat Road, and just before Juniper Campground take the Juniper Trail, Summit Trail, and Green Ranch Road to the site of the former Green Ranch. Descend on Alder Creek Road, with a side trip to Frog Pond. Return to trailhead via Frog Pond and Curry Canyon Roads. A total climb of 3200 feet, and 17.4 miles of hiking await you!

Description: This is a long, tough hike for expert map readers who have a good instinct for following faint trails, and is an exhilarating scramble up and down the flanks of the mountain.

7 BURMA ROAD LOOP

Trailhead: Not long after your car starts its climb on North Gate Road, you will note a distant ridge that comes in from the right to meet the winding road. After a particularly sharp curve, the highway rises steeply toward the ridge, access to which is provided by two bright aluminum gates on opposite sides of the road, just after the white 3.0 mile marker. Limited parking is available in front of the lower (western) gate or at a pullout just beyond. The trail starts at the upper (eastern) gate. No facilities.

Trail Statistics: Follow Burma Road beyond Moses Rock Spring, then descend on Burma Spring Trail to Mothers Trail, which ends at Angel Kerley Road. This shortly joins Burma Road, which takes you back to the trailhead. A 4.2-mile loop, 1260-ft. climb.

Description: After an astoundingly steep (but not very long) climb, Burma Road—named for the WWII mountainous supply route) gradually traverses Long Ridge and crosses a broad band of serpentine and peridotite with its weird rocks and stunted plants, a wildly barren stretch which contrasts with the lush grasses on the slumpy slopes. This is also a great birding area: rough-legged hawks, ash-throated fly-catchers, horned larks. At Moses Rock, a biblical spring issues from a crevice. Scramble to the top of the rock and find a little throne from which to lord it over the encompassing domain of beauty.

8 OYSTER POINT VIA RIGGS CANYON

Trailhead: On Morgan Territory Road heading toward Livermore, about four-and-a-half miles from Marsh Creek Road junction, just 0.4 miles beyond the two narrow one-lane bridges. There is a corral on the left side of the road, opposite the State Park pedestrian gate. There is a little space to park, but do not block the road gate; it is used by inholders. No facilities.

Trail Statistics: At the entrance, take the road that goes straight ahead. Continue up to Highland Ridge, turn left, and then right, descending into Riggs Canyon along a maze of unnamed roads. Take Oyster Point Trail to the destination. Round trip is 11.3 miles, with a total climb of 2660 feet.

Description: This is an exploration of some of the least visited parts of the park. Riggs Canyon is a mysterious Shangri-La, a deep valley of unspoiled wilderness, ringed by sandstone walls and weirdly eroded spires. The final climb to the Oyster Point ridge and its wonderful vistas is cross-country; watch out for poison oak. On the return trip, take a right on the Highland Ridge Trail and take the right-hand road back to the trailhead along the crest of grassy hills offering splendid distant views of Mt. Diablo.

9 GRAND LOOP

Trailhead: Lower Parking Lot, Summit. Facilities.

Trail Statistics: Start by descending the Summit Trail to Devil's Elbow. For the complete loop, take left turns at each junction: North Peak Trail to Prospectors Gap, Bald Ridge Trail to Murchio Gap, Meridian Ridge Road and then Deer Flat Road to Juniper Campground, and back up on the Juniper Trail. 6.8 miles with a total climb of 1820 feet.

Description: This is a circumambulation of the summit along some of the park's most attractive hidden trails. The North Peak Trail has fantastic displays of wildflowers in the spring, including the rarely seen wind poppies. The Bald Ridge Trail has a new surprise every few yards —a tiny rock garden, an unexpected vista, perhaps a sighting of the elusive California thrasher. The Meridian Ridge Road is a gem, an exploration of the geology and rare botany of serpentine soils and rocks. And the Juniper Trail has its own set of rock gardens featuring tundra-like stunted plants.

10 MT. OLYMPIA FROM THREE SPRINGS

Trailhead: Wide pull-out on right side of Marsh Creek Road about two miles beyond Regency Drive in Clayton. There is an emergency call box with a big blue sign. No facilities.

Trail Statistics: Turn right at first road junction and soon thereafter right onto a small trail. At its end make a short left jog on the gated road to locate the posted Olympia Trail. Follow it and its continuation, the East Trail, to the summit. The round trip is 5 miles, with a stiff 2200-foot climb.

Description: This is arguably the steepest trail in the park. The first part is gentle enough, but things get a lot more challenging when you get to the flanks of Mt. Olympia—the total rise occurs in a little over a mile. There are many things to attract your attention on the way and to let you catch your breath—wildflowers well into summer, grotesquely eroded rock formations reminiscent of the American Southwest, the sequence of gradually expanding views. The climax view, of course, is from the summit itself.

biking, riding, etc.

biking

A great way to explore Mt. Diablo State Park is on a mountain bike. You can cover a lot of ground, you typically don't have to drive into the park, and you can access some more difficult-to-reach places. But be forewarned—the steep terrain is best suited for experienced riders or those open to a challenge. The good news for beginning riders is that if you get in over your head, you can usually turn back and head downhill. Rides range from short out-and-backs at the lower elevations, to full-day rides with thousands of feet of vertical gain.

A few of the basics that riders should be aware of:

- Mountain bikes are permitted on all paved and fire roads within the park.

- Cross-country riding is highly offensive and illegal.

- A number of single-track trails are open to bikes and are typically signed with the prominent triangular multi-use signs. It is a biker's responsibility to know if the trail they are on is open to bikes. A current list of multi-use trails is:

  - All parts of the Summit Trail from South Gate entrance/ Dan Cook Canyon to Old Pioneer Horse Camp. Summit trail is closed to bikes beyond Old Pioneer Horse Camp.

  - Mothers Trail between Angel Kerley Fire Road and Burma Fire Road (uphill direction not recommended).

  - North Peak Trail between Summit Road–Devil's Elbow

turnout and Prospectors Gap (not recommended for beginners).

- Oyster Point Trail
- Diablo Ranch Trail
- Buckeye Trail

Locals use winter riding entrances at Mitchell Canyon and Dan Cook Canyon. The upper elevations are rideable during the rainy season, but the trail options are few, so many will ride the road to the top. Places to avoid in wet conditions due to sticky clay are Curry Canyon, Shell Ridge, Macedo Ranch, Pine Canyon, and Donner Canyon.

Bicyclists are advised to carry a map, such as the Trail Map of Mount Diablo State Park published by MDIA and available for $5 at many Bay Area bike stores, or at park entrance stations (North Gate and South Gate), the Summit Visitor Center, Mitchell Canyon Interpretive Center, and the Diablo Sector Office in Mitchell Canyon. Remember that you share the backcountry with hikers and horseback riders, so pass with care. Let others know of your presence—use a handlebar chime or an audible greeting. Always yield to horseback riders and when approaching ask the rider for directions; it may be necessary to dismount. A good rule of thumb, particularly when riding downhill, is to go slow enough to make conversation and eye contact, and be able to stop calmly if the situation warrants.

recommended rides

The best way to ride the mountain is to ride from your house or from one of the lower-elevation entrances. Driving into the park is time-consuming, and most riders avoid it. Below is a list of parking locations and rides.

PARKING LOCATIONS

From Clayton: Mitchell Canyon, Donner Canyon/Regency Drive, or downtown Clayton.

From Walnut Creek: Castle Rock Road, Borges Ranch, Walnut Creek BART station, the end of Marshall Drive/Shell Ridge, or Howe Homestead Park.

From Alamo/Danville: Livorna Staging at the east end of Livorna Road, Macedo Ranch, or Monte Vista High School (ride surface streets to Macedo Ranch or through Diablo to South Gate Road). Monte Vista High School is an excellent staging area for Rock City, Oyster Point, Knobcone Point, Green Ranch, and summit rides.

From Blackhawk: ½ mile before the end of Finley Road.

EASY RIDES

Generally, the nearer the summit, the harder the ride. If you're not looking for a real workout, it's best to stick to lower elevations.

- Try starting at the Macedo Ranch staging area at the north end of Green Valley Road in Alamo and ride five miles on the Briones–Mt. Diablo Trail to Marshall Drive in Shell Ridge. Except for a steep climb at the beginning on Wall Point Road it is relatively easy going thereafter.

- Shell Ridge provides excellent rides for beginners and those looking for less elevation gain. Enter via Marshall Drive or Howe Homestead. Ride out and back to Macedo Ranch—there is ample opportunity to explore side trails into Pine Canyon or out to Walnut Creek surface streets. Great views of Mount Diablo are obtained along the Briones Mt. Diablo Trail.

- Pine Canyon from Walnut Creek's Las Lomas High School or Castle Rock Park.

- An easy ride can also be had by going a couple of miles up Pine, Mitchell, and Donner Canyons; just turn around when the grade becomes too steep. Paved trails connect Donner Canyon with Clayton downtown.

INTERMEDIATE RIDES
- Rock City Loop I: Rock City to Pine Canyon via Wall Point Fire Road, up Pine Canyon to Barbecue Terrace Group Camp, short distance on Summit Road to Summit Trail, back down to Rock City. About seven miles; tough climb out of Pine Canyon to Barbecue Terrace.

- Rock City Loop II: up Wall Point, down Barbecue Terrace.

- Rocky City Loop III (most difficult): up Barbecue Terrace, down Wall Point.

Note: the Rock City loops can be made longer by parking in Walnut Creek or Castle Rock areas or by riding out and back from Curry Point to the park boundary along the Knobcone Point Fire Road.

- Mitchell Canyon to Deer Flat, or up to the grass ridge line of Moses

Rock Ridge, or Juniper Campground; return via same route or via Meridian Ridge Fire Road.

- Morgan Territory/Highland Ridge from Finley Road entrance—beautiful views of Mt. Diablo from the southeast.

EXTENDED AND ADVANCED RIDES

- Juniper Camp to Devils Elbow on Summit Road (paved), down North Peak Trail to Prospectors Gap, then fire roads from Prospectors Gap, along Meridian Ridge, to Deer Flat, and back to Juniper. About six miles. North Peak Trail descent requires technical skills.

- Up Barbecue Terrace to Summit Trail to Juniper campground, return same direction or descend Burma Road into Pine Canyon.

- Green Ranch/Frog Pond Loop (from Walnut Creek, Danville, or Alamo). Ascend summit trail to Old Pioneer Horse Camp, descend along fire roads, passing through abandoned Green Ranch, side trip to Frog Pond, into Curry Canyon. Great springtime ride when roads are dry and flowers are in full bloom. Ascend back to Curry Point. This is the one (loop) ride that bikers may want to drive into the park for, via the South Gate entrance—park at Curry Point or Rock City. An alternate shorter way to see the spring wildflowers is to ride out and back to Frog Pond via Curry Canyon—but reverse the route if you want to do the whole loop. Green Ranch is an excellent location to stop for a lunch break.

- Oyster Point from Danville/Alamo/Walnut Creek, return via same direction or, for easier return, exit Finley Road entrance and return via surface streets.

- Ride to the summit from any of the low-elevation entrances. Note that riding the paved road is required above the intersection of the Summit Trail and Summit Road below the Old Pioneer Horse Camp entrance. Danville and Walnut Creek riders have alternate descent of Burma Road from Juniper campground. Clayton-side riders can loop back via the North Peak Trail, Prospectors Gap, and Meridian Ridge.

HUGE RIDES

- The entire Diablo Trail which extends from Howe Homestead Park to Round Valley. An epic 32-mile point-to-point ride requiring car shuttle. Only two paved roads are crossed. The basic idea is to ride from Round Valley into Morgan Territory, cross Morgan Territory Road and ascend Highland Ridge, descend into Riggs Canyon, ride Oyster point to Curry Point, then take Wall Point and Mt. Diablo/Briones trail and exit Shell Ridge via Howe Homestead.

- From Walnut Creek/Alamo/Danville, ascend the summit and North Peak, with a return via Deer Flat and Juniper campground.

Additional notes:

Riding uphill is not recommended on the Burma Road uphill of North Gate Road, Mothers Trail, or Frog Pond.

Water is available at the summit, Rock City, Juniper Campground, and at many of the picnic areas located along the paved roads. No water is available along Finley Road.

For more information, check out the Bicycle Trails Council of the East Bay's website, www.btceastbay.org. In addition, the Diablo Cyclists group organizes a Wednesday-evening road ride on North Gate Road to the summit, and occasional mountain bike excursions. For a schedule of group rides, call (925) 274-3422 or visit www.diablocyclists.com.

horseback riding

Mount Diablo and Contra Costa have been horse country for over 200 years—from the days of the Spanish expeditions to Alta California in 1772 and 1776, through the 1940s when the inland East Bay was largely agricultural, up to present-day recreational riding.

The main staging areas for horses are Mitchell Canyon, Macedo Ranch, Curry Point, and the intersection of Morgan Territory and Marsh Creek Roads. Barbecue Terrace has overnight facilities for horses. Horses are allowed on all mountain trails with the exception of the Fire Interpretive Trail, and the Summit Trail above the lower summit parking lot. Most of the park's numerous springs, creeks, and streams dry up by early summer, but there are water troughs at Deer Flat, Juniper Camp, and Barbecue Terrace, and additional drinking fountains (bring a scoop or collapsible bucket) at Rock City and at the summit parking lot. Riders are encouraged to carry water for themselves.

Generally, the less steep trails are found on the western slope of Mt. Diablo where there are more foothill areas. The mountain's north- and east-side trails tend to be steeper and rockier overall, but this has a silver lining as drainage here is excellent and even during wet winter weather the fireroads hold up well as equestrian trails.

Riders should wear a hat or helmet, a long-sleeved shirt to ward off brambles and poison oak; bring flyspray for their horse depending on the season, a pocketknife/hoof pick, and something to eat. Remember that there is no grazing on the mountain (and dogs are not allowed on the trails).

Guided rides through the park are available from Western Trail Ride Adventures in Walnut Creek: www.westerntrailride.com, (925) 946-1475.

fire on the mountain

The plant communities of Mt. Diablo are meant to burn. Many chaparral plants respond well after a fire. Many, in fact, thrive on it, such as poison oak and yerba santa, with their oily, waxy leaves that assist in moisture retention but are also highly flammable. Both species are excellent sprouters following the passage of a fire. Knobcone pine (there is a stand above Blackhawk) requires fire for regeneration; the cones of the Knobcone open through exposure to intense heat.

Prior to the Euro-American settlement of the West, fires ignited by lightning burned without interference. These fires reduced fuel loads and played a major role in the plant communities of the West. Hence, the suppression of lightning fires has resulted in tremendous increases in fuel loads and contributed to the ferocious quality of many notable fire incidents. The last major conflagration was in August 1977 and burned 6000 acres. The Fire Interpretive Trail around the summit was built in its wake and features many fire species.

To reintroduce fire into the landscape while reducing their ferocity, managers of the State Park have implemented the use of prescribed fire. Prescribed fire is the application of fire onto a landscape under controlled conditions.

The prescribed fire program at Mt. Diablo began in 1986. A number of acres throughout the park have been targeted. A 1997 prescribed fire near Knobcone Point was directed at a Knobcone forest and expanse of chaparral that had no record of fire in the past century. That same year, a prescribed burn took place in the Little Pine Canyon area that was a part of a native plant regeneration project. A recent series of prescribed burns near Curry Point has demonstrated their effectiveness in reducing the regeneration of the obnoxious yellow star thistle.

Visitors to the park during fire season (roughly June through October) should note the Fire Danger Reading posted at the North Gate and South Gate entrances, at Macedo Ranch and Mitchell Canyon Staging Areas, and at all campgrounds. The fire-danger matrix below indicates the restrictions that apply depending on whether the risk of fire is judged to be low, medium, high, red flag, or very high/extreme.

fire danger reading	wood fires permitted	use of compressed logs	use of charcoal*	use of self-contained stove	cigarette smoking†	park closed‡
low	YES	YES	YES	YES	YES	NO
medium	NO	YES	YES	YES	YES	NO
high	NO	NO	YES	YES	NO	NO
red flag	NO	NO	NO	YES	NO	NO
very high/extreme	NO	NO	NO	NO	NO	NO

* The use of charcoal is not permitted during "Red Flag" fire alerts.
† The prohibition of smoking under high fire danger includes smoking within a vehicle.
‡ Park closure applies to all persons, vehicles, bicyclists (mountain and road), and horseback riders.

towers

There currently are seven towers on Mt. Diablo, three on the main peak and four on North Peak. Most function as communication repeaters, i.e. they amplify and relay local TV, radio, and cell-phone signals. Because they are located on peaks they are highly visible, and one of the goals articulated in the State Park's 1989 General Plan is that all the towers eventually be removed. Recently two towers were taken down, the Chevron tower on North Peak, in 1999, and, in 2001, AT&T's tower just below the summit, immediately adjacent to the Juniper Trail.

index